BODY LANGUAGE OF PEOPLE

How to Analyze People, Beginners Guide

Table of Contents

Introduction

Body language is a notion, which men and women effectively know well. The analysis and concept of it become popular in later years since we can comprehend what we stated during our bodily gestures and facial expressions, to interpret and show our inherent feelings and perspectives. Body language can also be known as 'non-verbal communications', and much less generally 'on-vocal communications. The term 'same-sex' will be utilized at a broader awareness, and each of these conditions is somewhat obscure. For this guide, the terms' body language' and 'non-verbal communications are widely interchangeable. This manual also has the view it is the analysis of how people communicate facial besides the spoken words. In this regard, the treatment of this topic here is more comprehensive than standard guides, that are restricted only to human gestures and positions. If you execute any serious analysis or debate, you should explain the language on your way.

Body language that is does comprise attention and facial expression movement. – Typically, what about perspiration and breathing? - This is dependent upon the definition used. And while pitch and tone of voice signs; is such part of body language? Not usually, but so if considering bodily gestures/expressions and just the phrases, because they could ignore by you. There are no replies to those questions. It is an issue of interpretation. For broadening our range, a reason is to avoid missing necessary signals which may not be contemplated inside a narrower definition. Nevertheless, confusion arises if definitions and context aren't correctly created, for instance: It's carelessly and commonly quoted that 'on-verbal communications' or 'body language' accounts for as many as 93 percent of their significance that individuals take from any personal communication. This is a simulation-based on the study concept, which while it is something of a basis of body language

5

study didn't create such a claim of Albert Mehrabian. Mehrabian's research findings centered on communications with a strong psychological or' feelings' component besides, the 93% non-verbal percentage included vocal intonation (paralinguistic), which can be considered by most as falling out the definition. When saying specific care must be resolved figures concerning proportions of conveyed, or in making any company claims concerning communications and body language. It's safe to state that body language signifies a huge percentage of meaning that is conveyed and translated between individuals. Resources and body language specialists appear to agree that between 50-80percent of communications are non-invasive. So, while the data was a change based on the circumstances, it is usually accepted that non-invasive communications are essential in the way we know each other. When we meet somebody for body language, it is particularly crucial the very first moment. We create, and this evaluation relies far more on what we believe in and see about another person that they speak. We produce an opinion about an individual that is brand new before they speak a word. This is quite powerful in forming impressions on meeting somebody. The result occurs both ways - from when we meet with somebody for the very first-time language, the unconscious and conscious levels determine our perception of them.

When someone meets with us, they form their impression from our signs most of us. And this influence continues throughout communications and relationships between individuals. Body language translated and is continually being exchanged on a subconscious level; this is occurring Involving individuals of this time. Remember - while you're interpreting (consciously or unconsciously) yours is continuously interpreted by the body language of individuals, so men and women. The individuals and, with the awareness of abilities body language often get an edge over those whose admiration is restricted to the subconscious. You may change your consciousness from the unconscious mindful by studying the topic, and then by practicing, you're studying communications on your dealings with other people.

Chapter 1:   Understanding Body Language

What Is Body Language?

Body language is utilized mainly to express sentiments. For example, if we are enamored with somebody, it is regularly hard to state that legitimately to the individual. It is, then again, simpler to make our sentiments unmistakable (purposefully or unexpectedly) through non-verbal communication. The inverse is likewise valid. We may state that we ARE irate through words, yet our body language might say loud and clear that we are NOT. This can be extremely confounding for the recipient of the message. The circumstance is usually portrayed as giving out twofold messages - one message in words and a contrary message in non-verbal communication. It is likewise hard to lie or conceal our emotions through non-verbal communication. We may give their actual sentiments away by not monitoring their non-verbal communication. Research has demonstrated that the vast majority give more consideration to, and accept all the more promptly, their impression of an individual's demonstrations through body language than what is said through words. As a result, we will, in general, be uncertain, or put a question mark behind the expressed words if they don't comply with the body language.

One of the most compelling methods of communication we use in our everyday collaborations is our non-verbal communication. It is the method of communication that lights our "gut-level" feelings and reactions. Research has shown that obtaining a profound comprehension of the body language builds one's capacity to be fruitful at getting anything one looks for from some random circumstance.

Have you at any point watched a couple sitting together and in minutes known how fortunate or unfortunate their relationship was? Did you ever consider how you had the option to arrive at this resolution so rapidly with no immediate connection? Even if you know about it or not, we go through our days, reacting to individuals' non-verbal signs communicated through their body language and reaching determinations about them from our perceptions.

Our body language uncovers the reality we conceal with our words from the world, including how we truly feel about ourselves, our connections, and our circumstances. Through our eye-to-eye connection, motions, body position, and outward appearances, the individuals we interact with can predict our aims.

The intensity of body language is found in the enthusiastic reaction it makes. Sentiments drive choices and responses in for all intents and purposes of each circumstance. Non-verbal signals trigger emotions that decide center resources of an individual, for example, honesty, dependability, earnestness, expertise level, and initiative capacities. The translation of these prompts can figure out who we date, the activity we get employed for, what level of progress we get, and even who might be chosen into influential political positions.

With such a significant ability, why don't we go through years of learning and creating viable body language aptitudes? The fact of the matter is that a great number of people underestimate the significance of body language until they are searching for a more profound comprehension of human conduct in an individual relationship, or increasing an edge in a focused business circumstance.

The dominance of body language gives individuals the keys to translate the importance behind clear signals and body development, just as providing a comprehension on the most proficient method to extend and impart messages adequately when managing others. Thus, generally speaking, adequacy in relational connections is extraordinarily expanded. The ideal approach to start this procedure of dominance is to get familiar with the fundamental understanding of the two center body language types - open nearness and shut nearness.

The shut nearness body language type is highlighted in people who overlay their bodies around the inside line, which runs straight down the center of the body from the highest point of the head to the feet. The physical qualities which make this sort of essence are: feet set near one another, arms held near the body, hands crossed on the body or held together before the body, little hand motions held near the body, shoulders moved forward, and eyes centered underneath eye level.

The messages conveyed to the world by the shut nearness sort of body language is an absence of certainty, low confidence, weakness, and an absence of experience. In extreme cases, one can even make the message of needing to be undetectable. The impacts on the individual with this kind of body language can extend from just not accepting the ideal chances to the direst outcome imaginable of harboring an inevitable perspective on exploitation.

Conversely, the open nearness is highlighted in people who make a feeling of power, and authority by displaying certainty, achievement, quality, and aptitude dominance. The physical attributes are: feet held up and widely separated, open hand signals utilized in discussion away from focus line of the body, elbows held away from the body, shoulders kept down, straight positions, and eyes centered at the eye level of the audience. These people are viewed as alluring, fruitful, savvy, and seem to have achievement come effectively. We see this body language type as the "body language of pioneers."

The eye-to-eye connection is the key to improve body language and begin to broaden open proximity. Eye-to-eye connection is one of the most significant specialized instruments we possess. By utilizing direct eye-to-eye connection when associating with others, one can change how other people view them. At the point when individuals start to talk and look directly into the audience's eyes, they are viewed as specific, dependable, and talented.

Hand motions and outward appearance are the second degree of progress one can make to be seen as open nearness—these methods of correspondence loan themselves to expanding the capacity to convey messages plainly and successfully. By utilizing freehand motions from the body and expressive facial influence skillfully, the more remarkable effect is made when talking by winding up more outwardly, animating to the audience, and expanding the measure of data gave during the cooperation.

The dominance of body language is crucial to making the best nearness in every single relational cooperation. People without this dominance are inclined to be misjudged and discover their endeavors to convey their thoughts fruitlessly. With the ability to differentiate between the various methods of non-verbal communication, anybody can successfully accomplish the dominance essential to wind up effective in whichever try they pick.

Body language is the most overlooked type of non-verbal communication. Well, the appropriate response is relatively straightforward. In what manner can an individual value something that they don't comprehend or realize how to use?

Do you understand who the guiltiest party is? Before you sign in to your email, think about one inquiry. Which sex uses body language the most, and in the entirety of its structures? The appropriate response is females. If they use it more often, guys, at that point, would presumably have a superior eye for non-verbal communication. A guy's first device to start body language is his eyes, which are typically joined by unpretentious face motions. This is the reason guys will, in general, be better at it than females. Then again, females utilize every one of the types of non-verbal communication. Not to say that guys don't. However, it isn't as healthy.

Ladies are the 'aces' of non-verbal communication. The sort of body language utilized by ladies relies upon the character of that particular lady. Timid and calm ladies, use progressively unobtrusive types of non-verbal communication, which makes it hard to tell whether body language is being utilized. With this sort of lady, the underlying peruses are hard. If you become acquainted with that lady at that point, after some time of comfort while expelling this powerlessness, and to create some understandable non-verbal communication. An out-going and perky lady isn't unpretentious at all with regards to utilizing non-verbal communication. They use it more often and is anything but difficult to take note. They are incredibly coquettish with their non-verbal correspondence and could heighten to slight stroking.

Body Contour

Ladies that regularly utilize this have a soft, well-proportioned body. They use the shapes of their body to tell how they are feeling. They attempt to build the curve of their body to intensify their effect on the individual who they are trying to catch their eye. This is an undisputed top choice since it shows off the characteristic magnificence of a lady's body, like that of a model. For what reason did I begin with the body? Studies demonstrate that the primary judgment a male pass on a female without seeing facial highlights is the body.

If they don't care for what they see, at that point, they move onto another lady. In any case, if they do, they move onto different resources of the bosoms and backside. Women, when I state, "If they don't care for what they see," this isn't escaping to body type, various men have various tastes along these lines. If you don't accommodate their criteria, at that point, they proceed onward. My perspective is that every lady is exceptionally delightful; it just takes the right person to find it.

Body Position

If a lady is hesitant about her body, she will utilize what she believes is the best resource she has. She may employ her bosom, backside, or even legs. Actually, this all depends upon the inclination of the lady too. A few men prefer one resource to another, and this can determine whether a man shows enthusiasm back to your non-verbal communication or not. Ladies that like to display their bosoms will wear low profile shirts, those that want to display their backside will wear more tightly pants, and those that like to show their legs will wear a skirt or something to that effect

For men, it is an entirely unexpected ball game. They don't show their skin except if at the shoreline, nor will they attempt to make body signals since guys' bodies were not programmed for that. Men mainly utilize their eye language to convey non-verbally. Be that as it may, the distinction here is whether the man has the CONFIDENCE to start or return non-verbal signals. Initially, a lot of men need certainty, so this in itself isn't amazing. The principal motivation behind why men are not happy with starting body language is because they are not positive about their ability to get it or how to give it back. So, they will simply stay away, except if they are affected by alcohol, which is a moment that is certainly not supported.

Notwithstanding, if you experience a man that shows it back, however, is utterly repulsive at it, give him a chance since this is effectively fixable. It is simpler to teach a man body language than it is to show them how to be sure. Like this, consider yourself an educator, and you are teaching your student, the man, how to start appropriate non-verbal communication just as it enables the man to realize what to search for later on with the goal that they are not as confused.

Chapter 2:   Verbal Communication VS Nonverbal Communication

Communication

It is generally believed that communication is an essential part of human behavior, but now, it is becoming evident that a lot of communication channels happens through nonverbal means. You look at someone and get the message they are passing across, you see a woman snap her fingers, and you get the message or an idea of what she's trying to say. It is a social infusion of interaction with a primary context of information flowing through knowledge in the human habitat. It activates the passing of news or messages to an extent where interpretation is needed to prove the coherence of a message.

Communication occurs after signals move from one channel point to the other, carrying information-related content between senders to the receiver through a communication chain. As much as language is needed for communication to have a balance substance in precision, it is, a matter of importance to understand the message in between. Style strengthens the communication system and allows humans to choose their words or signals, which might be in the generality of coded signals. Meanwhile, there is a seeming connection between what is said and what is heard. And at times, there is never what is heard, which is why nonverbal means of communication are in fashion too.

Verbal Communication

Communication systems employ the signs and symbols for interaction purposes. Assigns are signals used to convey a message, so it also is the general philosophy of verbal communication. Getting the whole idea of verbal communication and translating them right is a function of the receiver knowing the cause of the action. How do I mean? You get to understand a particular signal because you know the purpose of the work. For example, if your child mutters some words and points directly at the door, what does that mean? It means that probably someone is at the door or attention is need at the door. On the other hand, symbols are marks or words indicating a sophisticated level of reasoning and understanding between the parties involved. Symbols as complex as they seem brings about the concept of symbolic interactionism theory.

Whenever verbal communication takes place, it allows us to look for and understand the symbolic content that gives us the idea of what the speaker is talking about. This process is sub-divided into:

Semanticity: Semanticity knows the relationship between the after-effect of action and what caused it. As you know that signals stand for a particular meaning of its own even though it might be construed to mean other complicated things. For example, A little child shouting at the top of his voice with a sharp knife in his hand connotes something. So as an observer, what comes to your mind is that he cut himself with the sword and not that his noise stands outrightly for the cut itself. It allows you to see occurrences differently as much as you see it separately to understand the central message it's passing across.

Generativity: Generativity takes the stand that a finite message could take the shape of infinite meanings. The idea shows the level at which diverse thoughts range from individual to individual. And that's why languages are capable of combining and recombining symbols and signals to produce meaningful and comprehensible utterances to users of the word.

Displacement: this third pillar supports the idea of communicating what is abstract, and it has a linkage in language. This is because style gives room for the communication of things that exists only in mind. The artistic tendencies through this displacement factor allow communicating participants to discuss that which only exists in the imagination aside from what can be seen.

Nonverbal Communication

Nonverbal communication is a very vital medium of communication that gives room for sending and receiving messages using any of the human sensory organs without the use of words or utterances. There are several forms of nonverbal communication, and they include body language, facial expressions, posture, and gestures, and so on. The purpose of these cues is to pass across information through the movement of some parts of the body which have interpretations to them based on individuality complex.

Nonverbal Cues

Nonverbal cues are informative behaviors that are not entirely linguistic as far as the content of the message is concerned. And for the visible nonverbal cues, there are head movements, facial expressions, hand and body movements, etc. all these have a direct relationship with the interpersonal communication and the long-term effect it has in bringing people together.

While on the other hand, auditory nonverbal cues deal with nonlinguistic sounds as related to pitches and its variations, how loud it is, the speed it takes, and also breathiness. The study of nonverbal behavior has a linkage in some aspects of psychology, which reflects the nature of human, social impact, differences between groups and individuals. However, to understand and thoroughly analyze people, there is a need to draw a line between nonverbal behavior and nonverbal communication because they are two distinct concepts. While nonverbal behavior includes actions that ensue without the awareness of the person conveying the message, nonverbal communication also deals with the same as they could be used interchangeably.

Interpreting Nonverbal Cues

It is possible to understand nonverbal cues, whether the right way or wrongly, and this gives room for misunderstanding. As you send a message, there may be leakage, which is the unintentional transmission of information through nonverbal channels.

As noted, before, nonverbal cues have tendencies to be misinterpreted due to the ambiguous translations attached to them. So, for you to get a clue of what is being said, you'll need other information before you get the correct interpretation. These cues are mainly to serve the function of conveying emotions, interpersonal attitudes, or any related habits to pass a message across. That is why nonverbal cues serve as a way of giving feedback to what another person said to show how comprehending the message seems. So, with these cues, you can comment, dramatize, or react to any discussion without having to say a word.

However, the art of analyzing people comes with the need to understand the coordination of these behaviors. Nonverbal behaviors foster a sort of intimacy between people, thereby helping them maintain relationships in the long run or a desired level of rapport. Another essential side to nonverbal behaviors is how you present yourself. How do you introduce yourself before someone? What was the first impression that spurred from you to the other person? How would you react if you were in the person's shoes? These and many more questions give way for a better comprehension of what the appropriate relationship or communication should be. It further gives you an idea for the kind of expressions that are needed per time or knowing the phrases that best suit someone and the best time to do that. So, you're expected to understand the emotional situation at hand and how best to react to it in social parlance. This sense of self-presentation involves all these and more depending on how important you take human interactions daily.

Nonverbal cues, despite its ambiguous attachment of meanings, include blinking, finger movements, a smile, movement of the eyeballs in a particular direction, etc. You should, not be tempted to stand on what you perceive to be the meaning of each of these. When you smile, it might mean a sign of disapproval according to some cultures. The rising pitch of your voice shows that you're under stress, but the meaning might differ from another person. When you fold your arms, it might mean different thing to the person next to you, and that's how the chain goes on and on. So what do I do? You just have to take note of your baseline, the initial sign or signal, and the subsequent signals. However, there are generalizations of language and exceptions in them to behold, which doesn't change the stance of social influences of how people relate.

How to interpret Nonverbal communication.

While verbal communication uses language to explain external information and events, nonverbal communication plays a vital role in establishing and building an interpersonal relationship. Specifically, in human connection, nonverbal behavior helps in:

- expressing one's emotions

- presenting one's personality

- conveying attitudes

- facilitating speech for managing interaction cues between individuals and groups, and

Nonverbal Communication comes in different forms, and one must understand this before delving into interpreting it. You should always take cognizance of culture and language in the literary sense because these forms the basis of interpretation. For further studies, the following are examples of nonverbal communication that you should have full knowledge of and its straightforward understanding.

Chronemics: is an example of nonverbal communication that involves timing as a significant substance for discussion. At times, you wonder why a particular culture or person talks faster; this is a function of chronemics. The duration of time a person is willing to listen, the passage of intermediary information, the wait involved in communication, and the general timing of communication forms the basis of chronemics. This idea of chronemics makes you understand how the channel and timing of communication can vary in meaning depending on culture and individual personalities. So, to analyze people, you must consider this.

Haptics: This has to do with the physical contact that could arise through kissing, shoulder pads, arms beating, and head nodding, and so on. What shaking of hands means in another country might be different from what it says in the United States. That is why proper understanding, at least at the intermediary level, is needed to analyze people as the same thing goes for other salutations and how they're interpreted differently.

Kinesics: this includes body movement, facial expressions, eye contact, and to pass across messages. These movements have rich messages embedded in them, and as such, all body postures indicate a specific attitude towards the other person. All these cues show the extent of emotion attached to social information.

Chapter 3:   Origin of Body Language in Communication

Body Language in History

There are gestures, like the "manual rhetoric" of the Roman orators and the general mannerism of the entire body, that have been studied since Classical times. During the fourth century BCE in Greece, the upperclassmen kept what was considered a "firm" stance and an unhurried walk where they took long strides. This made them appear as people of leisure, which set them apart from slaves and artisans who always had to hurry to get things done. It also worked to separate them from women as well, who walked unnaturally and took small steps. The courtesans of the time would sway their hips as they walked. In Ancient Rome, strictly controlled and limited gestures made a person look in control, which was required for orators and aristocrats.

Writings about body language were prevalent during the Renaissance. The physiognomists of the 17th century, such as Charles Lebrun and Giovanni Della Porta, organized the facial expressions of different emotions and characters. There investigations on gestures, and the investigations of their contemporaries John Bulwer and Giovanni Bonifacio, were conducted by assuming there was a universal language of gesture and expression which people could assume and understand all around the world.

The chances are that the practical study of nonverbal communication started with actors. This is especially true during the 19th century when silent movies were first shown. Actors learned how to properly display feelings, status, and attitudes by mimicking the body language of their characters, which is no small feat.

The amazing things are that it is easy to understand and connect with the character even though there are no words or voices. This goes to show how powerful and relevant body language is.

Who Was the First Person to Study Body Language and Its Origins?

Charles Darwin, the father of evolution. He was the first person to start studying the body language of animals and humans in the book The Expression of the Emotions of Man and Animals in 1872. Through careful observation, he found that humans, much like animals, shared inborn behaviors that everybody used. These cues were able to reveal internal emotions or were able to help communicate with people.

The physical conditions that people had to live in, their bodily movements, and their frequent actions all had some sort of consequence on the structure of their bodies. This was discovered by paleo-archaeologists who used excavated skeletons to offer some thoughts about past body habits. There are some modern zoologists and ethnologists, like Desmond Morris, who stress the similarities of body movements between animals and humans when expressing dominance, fear, and hostility.

Through his book, he pretty much established the science of body language. The majority of observations and studies made today started with his studies.

The biggest parts of the study of non-verbal communication began, oddly enough, during the 1960s. Since that time, it has become a major part of different sciences like psychiatry, social science, anthropology, and business.

Albert Mehrabian

In the late '60s, Albert Mehrabian performed many experiments to try and figure out how important gestures and intonation were when it came to sharing messages. He found that about seven percent of our communication took place verbally. 39% of it he called paraverbal, which means tone and intonation, and the remaining 55% was nonverbal. This means that the movement of our body, hands, and other simple gestures are very important in the way that we communicate.

People do sometimes debate these results because it came from a controlled experiment and didn't reflect what would be considered a realistic setting. But it was able to give Mehrabian a chance to show the words alone will not provide us with enough information to understand a message.

- **Intonation**

Intonation refers to the varying pitch of a person's voice when they speak. Let's think about the word 'thanks.' This is typically seen as a positive word, right? However, if somebody were to say 'thanks' in a firm or curt tone, how are you going to feel? You probably aren't going to interpret it positively, and you probably won't believe that they are thankful at all. Intonation is a big part of how we convey emotions.

Facial expressions and intonation tend to be very similar across cultures. You can pretty much figure out when a person is disgusted no matter where you are in the world. Similarly, happiness and sadness are typically the same as the world over.

- **Gestures and Movements**

Gestures are a person's way of conveying the subtle parts of a message. Gestures can even take the place of entire words. For example, if you want a person to continue talking because what they are saying is interested, you won't cut them off and say, "That's cool! Keep talking." You are likely going to lean forward to let them know you are interested in the things they are saying, or you can nod your head. Most of our gestures involve our hands. In the US, hello tends to be said with a wave. A thumb up is used to say everything is good, or, if a person were to become extremely upset, we could use our middle finger. We can even display impatience with our hands.

Differences in Cultures

The modern study of body language is based on assuming that gestures aren't universal or natural. Instead, they are the products of culture and social influence. The likeness between facial expressions of chimps to show fear and subordination, and the smile of a human, can help to show the difference and the similarities between two primate species.

Anthropologists, like Marcel Mauss, have shown that even the smallest parts of physical activity, like how a person sits, walks, sleeps, or eats, seem to be affected by their culture and vary between societies. This includes not only deliberate signals people use for communication but also the involuntary reactions, like weeping or blushing.

Actions that may seem as intuitive or spontaneous, when looked at closely, are not transparent or spontaneous. To some degree, they are ordered, formalized, and stylized to a certain code, which could mean nothing in different cultures, places, or contexts. The person who she leaps to her feet, smiling, and hugs another person may create some type of discomfort or offense to a person who isn't familiar with this type of greeting. The action of simply nodding the head as you walk past may not have the same effect on a person who isn't used to displaying public acknowledgments.

Modern Studies

The majority of people who study body language are social psychologists, linguists, and anthropologists. The science of body language is kinesics. Their studies include the ways and frequency with which others touch people when they talk and the distance they have during their interactions. Linguists have called gestures as another form of language, possibly even the predecessor of language. They have studied several forms of kinesics communication used by different groups and cultures, like clergy, stockbrokers, and beggars.

Body language provides information that you can't get anywhere else in communication. Movements and expressions can modify, amplify, subvert, and confirm speech. It expresses meanings that may surpass or elude speech. This provides us with a way to see the inner emotional and psychological state of the speaker. Many years before Freud, early writers on decorum talked about slips shown through unintentional body movements, which would undermine or contradict the things they said.

Gestures are unique to the different rites and codes of various cultures. This means body language is important to fundamental assumptions and values. It gives a person a chance to move from nature into their culture through the demeanor and gestures which people use to express meaning, whether inadvertent or deliberate. There are many formal contexts where the speaker's movements and posture are more important than the words they say. Body language plays a big part in non-literate or semi-literate societies where they make commitments through ritual actions and other symbolic objects.

Shame and Purity

There are theories they try to explain why variations or changes in the body language take place. During the 1930s, Norbert Elias, a sociologist, suggested his argument that was based mostly on European Protestant sources. He suggested that after the freedom in the body language of the Middle Ages, early modern Europe had an increase of inhibition with their bodily impulses. This was seen in a rise in shame or embarrassment around physical movements, and a bigger concern over the control or restraint of actions and expressions of emotions.

Mary Douglas, an anthropologist, has argued that with most societies, the body is a social relations symbol, and controlling the body according to the customs of the society is more or less strict according to the peer pressure a person feels.

Surveys across cultures show the variability of gestures and expressions are supplemented by what travelers experience when they go to different countries, or even things seen in movies and heard in music from different areas of the world. There is a chance that with long-distance travel in the late 20th century and the globalization of culture, some differences have started to diminish. The homogenization of cultures can happen quickly in different aspects, like fashion, foods, or using foreign words or decorations. But it takes more time when it comes to gestures and expressions, which people take longer to absorb and change.

Body language is not only the most fundamental form of expression used by humans, but it is also a very sophisticated and culturally specific form of signals where movements and expressions play as much a part as speech. Its groups in the infant grimaces of distaste to an unpleasant sensation, the time of bows between Japanese people of equal rank, and the series of insulting hand gestures that altercating drivers share in Brazil.

Difficulties of Body Language

The people of America and Britain have similar body language, so people of those countries will find it easy to read each other.

There can still be some regional differences, but it still isn't that hard to figure certain things out. If from America or Britain, they would likely have a bit of a probably trying to understand the nonverbal language of other countries. If you went to Croatia and waved at somebody, you may be met with looks of scorn or worse because to them, that's offensive. They think it looks too much like a Nazi salute. Luckily for us, we have Google. If you are planning on traveling to other countries, doing a quick search for offensive body language may be a good idea and could keep you out of trouble.

Chapter 4:   Our Bodies and The Way They Speak

Bodily Gesture

There are different types of body language. This is because we cannot classify the different styles in the same category. Different body languages can be distinguished. So, which body language styles can be differentiated? Generally, the body language is divided into two columns. That includes; Body parts and the Intent

Let us start with the body parts and the language they communicate.

The Head - The placement of the head and its movement, back and forth, right to left, side to side, including the shake of hair.

Face - This includes facial expressions. You should note that the face has many muscles ranging from 54 and 98 whose work is to move different areas of the face.

The movements of the face depict the state of your mind.

- **Eyebrows** - The eyebrows can express themselves through moving up and down, as well as giving a frown

- **Eyes** - The eyes can be rolled, move up down, right, and left, blink as well as the dilatation

- **The Nose** - The expression of the nose can be by the flaring of the nostrils and the formation of wrinkles at the top

- **The Lips** - There are many roles played by the lips, that include snarling, smiling, kissing, opened, closed, tight, and puckering

- **The Tongue** - The tongue can roll in and out, go up and down, touch while kissing, and also the licking of lips

- **The Jaw** - The jaw opens and closes, it can be clinched and also the lower jaw can be moved right and left

- **Your Body Posture** - This describes the way you place your body, legs, and arms connected, and also concerning other people

- **The Body Proximity** - This looks at how far your body is to other people

- **Shoulder Movements** - They move up and down, get hunched, and hang

- **The Arm** - These go up down, straight and crossed

Legs and The Feet – these can have an expression in many different ways. They can be straight, crossed, legs placed one over the other, the feet can face the next person you are in a conversation with, they can face away from each other, the feet can be dangling the shoes

The Hand and The Fingers – the way that your hands and fingers move is powerful in reading other people's gestures. The hands can move up and down, they can do some hidden language that only people of the same group can understand.

How One Reacts to Handling and Placing of Objects – this is not regarded as a body part but it technically plays a role in reading a body language. This may predict anger, happiness and much more.

This includes willingly making body movements otherwise known as gestures. These are the movements that you intended to make for example shaking of hands, blinking your eyes, moving, and shaking your body in a sexy way maybe to lure someone and much more. There are also involuntary movements-this are movements that you have no control over. This can be sweating, laughter, crying and much more.

Descriptive Gestures

You will find people that move their hands around a lot, while others move them just a little bit. So, what is the right thing for you to do?

According to research, the people that move their hands around a lot are good speakers.

However, it is not all about moving your hands around aimlessly – you need to understand what each movement means and how you can make it work for you.

This is true because the right-hand signals will complement the words that come from your mouth.

You also explain a concept faster than before, because it is like sending a message using two explanations instead of the traditional one.

Emphatic Gestures

How often do we say, "If I were you," and I mean in reality, "If I, I were in one place like yours...?" It's not easy to feel what it's like in someone else's shoes. What do you think of the following rule?

Someone who cannot become aware of their own body language signals will never be able to register the signals of others very accurately. Body language analysis requires not only a "sharp" (read: trained) gaze and a "good" (i.e. trained) ear, but probably a much higher degree of good "sense."

This word describes a good empathy without which any method of self and human knowledge will fail. Registering one's own feelings and non-verbal signals means going through two essential processes:

First, one perceives a signal, e.g. For example, one tugs nervously on the lip. Second, you register how you feel right now. This combination helps one later tote others guess what feeling may have triggered a particular signal with them. Of course, this guessing is commonly called 'interpret' because it sounds 'scientific'. However, the fact remains that scientists must also "guess" as long as they work on a theory of knowledge, that is, create. Empathy for others can, therefore, be practiced by registering one's own processes. We can express this again as a rule:

The more empathy a person has with their own emotional world, the more they will be able to develop for others and vice versa. This rule also explains why especially sensitive people not only have much understanding for others but are also very sensitive (sometimes mimosa-like) to others.

Suggestive Gestures

Studies show that the way you hold your palms will say a lot about you.

When you have your palms facing upwards, you will show a positive behavior while palms facing downwards will show negative behavior.

Palms facing up tell the person that you are welcoming and honest.

For example, if you are negotiating with a salesperson when buying something and he is putting his palms facing upwards while saying he cannot go any lower than he is honest and you need to believe him.

If the palms are facing downwards, then he is more emphatic.

In the first instance you can keep on negotiating because he might go lower, but in the next instance, he won't go any lower.

It has also been known that those who talk without gesticulating are prone to talking lies than those that talk with a lot of gestures.

If you have watched a politician talk, then you must have realized that they usually use a lot of gestures than many people.

They also like to use open arm gestures to show some honesty.

Pointing is rare in most cases with politicians because they know that it is seen to be rude.

Prompting Gestures

Verbal and nonverbal cues determine how well you can communicate with people. It is about understanding the content and the context at the same time and communicating back in kind. Verbal cues are simple prompts in conversation that ask for your attention or need your response to something. They are very clear.

"Does anyone have the answer?"

This is a direct verbal cue prompting anyone who might have the correct answer to speak up. Everyone understands this. If you don't have the answer, you might probably look around the room to see who has so that you can be attentive and listen to their explanation. Verbal cues are straightforward and explicit. You cannot mistake them.

Direct verbal cues are clear, whether you are asking a question or giving instructions. The message is clear between the decoder and the sender of the message. There is a chronological order in which ideas are conveyed.

The difference with nonverbal cues? These are indirect. They are often implied but not explicit. Indirect verbal cues can be subtle. You have to be very keen to identify them. Given their complicated nature, they are often easy to misunderstand.

Indirect verbal cues are often affected by context. Instead of saying what they want, someone acts it out, hoping you can understand them without them having to say it out loud. Affiliation to different cultural groups, societies, and other interactions often affect the understanding of indirect verbal cues. It might not be easy to read verbal cues, but with some insight, you can hack it. Here are some useful tips:

Recognize Differences. You must first understand that people are different, and for this reason, their communication styles might not be similar to yours. Everyone responds to verbal cues differently. When you respect this, it is easier to create an environment where you can understand one another.

Overcoming Bias. The next thing you have to overcome is your personal bias. Everyone is biased over something in one way or the other. Most of the time, you are biased without even realizing it. This is because of inherent traits, beliefs, and core values that you live by. These affect the way you comprehend things or how you recognize challenges.

Some people who are used to direct verbal cues might find it difficult to interact with people who are used to indirect verbal cues. You might even assume them dishonest because they are not communicating in a manner you are used to. On their part, they might find you unassuming, difficult to deal with, and insensitive. Some might even feel offended, yet you both mean well.

Embrace Diversity. Effective communication is about embracing diversity. People show different emotions in different ways in different parts of the world. This might not be the same as what you are used to, but it is how they do things. It is wise to learn about cultural relations, especially if you might have a very diverse audience.

Practice. You can learn everything you don't know. Learning means setting aside time to practice and get used to people, styles, and so forth. Learning will help you to become flexible and understand the differences between your preferred style of communication and another person's.

Chapter 5:   Positive and Negative Body Gestures

Body language involves how we use our physical behavior, expressions, and manners to reveal nonverbal information about ourselves, which is usually done unconsciously. Many people are not aware of it, but in all your interactions, you are constantly giving out body cues and wordless signals that serve either to reinforce/solidify the interaction or to contradict what you are trying to say.

Your entire nonverbal behaviors transmit a loud and strong message that continues even after you stop talking. There are instances when what someone says might differ from what their body language is communicating. Hence, in this case, it will be easy for the person you are interacting with to pass you off as a liar. If someone asked for a favor and gave a frown after giving a no, you have ended up confusing the person. With this kind of mixed signal, the person might be confused about what to believe. However, if the person understands the concept of body language, he would probably just walk away since the body language is unconscious and gives someone out by revealing true intention.

Positive Body Language

A positive body language is welcoming, attractive, and full of confidence. Here are some body language cues that signal positivity:

Smile

A genuine, real, and appropriate smile carries a lot of power. It lifts the mood and is welcoming. It makes people feel better and lightens up the atmosphere. It is surely attractive as well. You have been eyeing a lady and stealing glances at her. Suddenly you made eye contact, and she smiled. That is a cue for you to know that you are welcomed.

Eye Contact

I sometimes remember a rift I had with my girlfriend. In a bid to resolve it, we had a face-to-face conversation. Throughout the conversation, she avoided my gaze. This was understandable and expected as she was mad at me. However, what I tried to do was get her to make eye contact with me. Eye contact creates some form of connection between two people. This is how important eye contact is.

Having a conversation with someone and looking them in the eye makes them feel important and valued. This is because eye contact signifies attention. If you are with someone and the person keeps glancing around or looking at their watch or their phone, it is a sure sign of lack of interest in the interaction.

The Right Posture

The posture of the person you are interacting with also carries a lot of meaning. A person standing or sitting straight, for instance, sends a positive message. This is different from a slouch, tensed, or unrelaxed posture. Someone who looks confident and relaxed will surely attract others to them.

In any interaction, pay attention to where the person leans. A person who leans toward you is definitely interested in the interaction and subject of discussion.

The head direction matters as well. A slight tilt of the head is a positive indication that the other party is curious and interested in the conversation.

The Right Touch

Touching makes people feel good as it releases endorphins. It should, however, be used appropriately and in the right context. A firm and warm handshake, for instance, indicate that you are welcomed. The same is true with a pat on the shoulder. A pat on the shoulder from your boss, for instance, is an indication that you have scored some good points.

The Direction of the Body

Pay attention to the direction the other person's body is facing. This signals whether you have their attention or not. A body or feet angled away gives the impression that the person wants to get away.

Personal Space

The distance and space between people are an indication of the level of relation between them. People in close proximity, say two to four feet are close friends or in a relationship. While a distance of about four to ten feet is for social interaction between people you are not very familiar with.

Nodding

Pay attention to the rate and frequency of nodding. A slow nod is a sign that someone is paying attention to you and interested in the conversation.

Mirroring

When a person is copying your body language, vocal speech, gestures, or pattern of body movement, there is a big chance you have established rapport.

Open Body Language

Pay attention to the arms and legs. As long as neither of them is crossed, the conversation or interaction is likely going in the right direction, and your partner is open to what you are saying.

Negative Body Language

There are negative body signals that show discomfort, hostility, anxiety, or a pure lack of interest. Pay attention to the following:

Tense

A tensed person is uncomfortable, which could be because of many things. You might have said something that turned them off, or perhaps you are standing too close to them. And better still, it could have nothing to do with you.

Fast Anxious Movements

If you are uncomfortable, the body is programmed to trigger you to flee the environment and situation. Hence, the pattern of speech, rate of movement, etc. of the other person indicate they are uncomfortable with you.

Desperately Trying to Be Still

Think about it. In a normal, relaxed setting, you are free. You move any part of your body unconsciously and without any resistance since there is nothing to worry about. However, watch out if the person sits still or is not gesticulating, especially if this is something they would normally do. It could point out to nervousness and discomfort that they are desperately trying to hide.

Lack of Eye Contact

If you are interested in something, your eyes will be fixed on that thing. It's not necessarily fixed, but much of your gaze will be directed at that thing. Hence, pay attention to the eyes of the person you are with. Looking away, lack of eye contact, looking at the floor or glancing on the watch are all negative body signals that show a lack of interest in the interaction.

Crossed Arms and Legs

While crossed arms and legs are a sign of defensiveness, they could also mean that the person feels cold, or perhaps they just find this position comfortable. However, it could also be that the person you are with is not interested in the interaction.

The same thing applies to cross the legs. Watch out for legs crossed with the knees pointing toward you. It is a pure negative sign.

These are the classic sign of a closed body language. Also, pay attention to where the other person is facing. Is it toward or away from you?

Body Pointing Away from You

Pay attention to the direction in which the torso, feet, and overall body are pointing. If any of this is away from you, the person has lost interest in the interaction. You might or might not be the cause of this body signal. For instance, in a board meeting, someone who keeps glancing at the door with the legs pointed toward the exit is bored and wants to leave.

Position of the Arms

Arms in the pocket or hands clasped in front of you give an impression that something is wrong.

Slouching

Your posture could also give out a positive or negative vibe, depending on what posture you put forth. Slouching, for instance, is a classic sign of lack of confidence.

Rubbing Any Body Part

People often do this when they are not comfortable. They could rub their fingers, neck, face, hair, or leg. It is a classic sign of discomfort when a person is not comfortable with the topic of discussion or is super nervous. It could also be someone hiding information, hence trying to keep themselves calm by such self-soothing behavior.

Barriers

When we are uncomfortable with the person we are talking to or the subject of discussion, there is a chance that we create a barrier between us. This barrier could be body parts, like the arms, legs, or objects. Someone who holds a briefcase tightly against their chest when communicating is clearly showing a blocking behavior.

Fidgeting

This is a classic sign of negative energy. Fidgeting is the body involuntarily trying to escape an uncomfortable situation. Examples are tapping of the feet and drumming of the hands. People could do this consciously or unconsciously when bored. It is also a sign of impatience with the person or conversation.

Chapter 6:   Body Language Myth – Facial Expression

In what ought to be an astonishment to nobody, the face likewise contains the most expressive non-verbal communication signals on the body. Except if somebody has put forth a coordinated attempt to examine, learn, and conquer every single subconscious development, how somebody's face looks and how individuals contact it'll frequently be a key to their internal contemplation and sentiments.

There's an explanation that the poker face is so prized and hard to learn, in any event, for the most expert and worthwhile of poker experts. It's the reason such a large number of them despite everything wear shades when they play poker. It's simply damn hard to not have a facial spasm or appearance that shows what somebody's truly thinking.

The amusing part about outward appearance is that many individuals feel that they recognize what the signs mean since they're so regular and far reaching.

Obviously, this presents a huge issue. Similarly, likewise with each other non-verbal communication signal, for example, crossing the arms, there's a huge amount of vagueness, absence of lucidity, and setting reliance in deciphering somebody's facial signals particularly with dear companions.

Facial expressions are often small, but detectable with awareness and a little bit of practice.

Unconscious Micro-expressions.

Micro expressions are facial expressions that we hardly realize that we're making. They usually also come from emotions that we want to hide, but aren't able to and people don't typically feel the need to hide the positive emotions.

In case you're foreseeing something lovely to occur, you'll likewise have a slight grin for a small amount of a second. The most well-known scopes of micro-expression are bliss, shock, appall, outrage, certainty, and solace, among numerous others. These micro-expressions are often developed after some time.

Obviously, individuals do some of the time notice micro-expression, however their own tendency makes them very hard to comprehend and decipher. In addition, a great deal of micro-expression is truly mixing of a wide range of facial signs.

You might be sending separate signs with your eyebrows, eyes, and grin, all joined into a progression of micro-expressions. So, by what method can break micro-expression into a smaller segment?

Eyebrows

Eyebrows are very expressive & an easy signal to read. Raised eyebrows are ordinarily indications of heightened awareness. If you are talking to someone and their eyebrows raise throughout the whole conversation, you've piqued their curiosity & said something to make them pay attention – for better or worse.

Beside increased mindfulness, raised eyebrows are frequently observed as an indication of friendliness and accommodation. It makes an impact of 'soft eyes,' and is to show that you intend no mischief, and come in peace. It's the sort of non-verbal communication signal you may unwittingly do when you're meeting another person, or moving toward a little dog.

This' certainly not a negative part of accommodation – it just messages that you need to be loved by others and that you aren't a danger of any sort. This' the sort of non-verbal communication signal that you need to convey to lubricate social circumstances, as effectively settling a business negotiation, or being a tease up a tempest.

A single raised eyebrow really has a different meaning than when the two eyebrows ascend simultaneously. A single raised eyebrow is much faster and momentary action, while the two eyebrows raised are something that is regularly held. This demonstrates some degree or doubt, shock, stun, or oddity. When in doubt, the feeling to concentrate on is shock at the uncover of something sudden, for positive or even negative.

At last, when you bring down your eyebrows, this' all around deciphered as threatening or undermining. As it were, you're irate or disturbed. At times, it can likewise be deciphered as you feeling miserable or feeling compromised.

Eye Direction.

We've all heard that strong eye contact – a good balance between strong eye contact & breaking it, is ideal for creating trust & empathy.

But we also all know that most people don't do this, & unconsciously move their eyes in directions that can indicate a range of the emotions that they're feeling.

You're not going to be able to read them completely, but the following guidelines have been shown to be tested & true.

If someone's moving their eyes upwards to the right, this usually means that they're trying to recall something from their memory. They're trying to recollect something that they've seen in the past, & redirect their eyes to try to scan their memory. This's typically harmless, unless it's paired with some body language signals that might indicate that there's a lie brewing.

However, if someone's talking & their eyes drift to the upper left, this will usually mean one of two things. First, they might be thinking something creative, and be thinking about how to express themselves artistically. You can also think of this mode as daydreaming.

Second, the eyes might drift to the upper left if they're actively lying to you. But of course, this's very contextual & best judged with paired with other signals.

You also have to take into account that studies have shown that visual people tend to look upwards while they're lying – because they're literally painting a fake memory for themselves to recite.

If they move their eyes to one side, they are simply basically attempting to recollect something that they have heard before. if they will move their eyes to the left while they are talking, they are simply attempting to imagine something that they have heard. Once more, this may lead to supporting a conclusion that the individual is lying. It simply all relies on the questions you ask them while they're talking.

Individuals who will in general glance at the lower corner of their eyes while talking are individuals who will in general explore their feelings. In the event that they just look to their lower right while they're talking, it implies that they are attempting to recollect something that they have felt, tasted, or smelled before. In the event that they are talking and they're looking to their lower left, they may be conversing with themselves. They are going into an internal dialogue

At last, a non-directional tip. In the event that somebody just gives off an impression of being squinting at you, it gives the sign of irritation or even wariness.

Glasses

One of the most widely recognized characteristics people have with regards to their face, and their eyes are their main event with their glasses. Many individuals reposition their glasses on their nose while they're talking. You may believe that it is innocent and harmless. But in reality, it is actually giving away a lot of their thinking processes.

Fortunately, when someone is repositioning their glasses while you're talking to them, it implies that they need to hear more.

Every time you are talking to people, you have to remember that they are focusing on more than the words that you are stating. In a lot of cases, your message is only interpreted based on the totality of the experience talking with you. This also involves your tone of voice, how energetic you are, your facial expressions, & your micro-expressions. If you want to be a more effective communicator, you have to be more aware of your micro-expressions, and control them in such a way that they lead to a consistent interpretation.

Chapter 7:   Body Mirroring

Have you ever sat in a restaurant and people watched? It can be quite amusing to sit back and watch all of the people out and about around you, attempting to identify how their relationships must be going by body language alone. Yes, it is quite possible to understand at the briefest glance at another how they get along. You can absolutely tell how much or how little people get along simply by watching them together and seeing how they naturally orient their bodies around each other. This simple skill is referred to as mirroring, and it is absolutely crucial if you want to be successful at influencing or persuading others. When you understand mirroring, you essentially have a built-in system in which you can judge just how well people are likely to be willing to listen to you. You can tell if you are successful in developing rapport, and if you have not, you will be able to push the act of earning rapport along a little quicker. You can utilize mirroring in a wide range of ways that can absolutely be beneficial to you, and you can utilize it in ways that can be useful to others as well.

What is Mirroring?

First things first, you must learn what mirroring is. At the simplest, it is the human tendency to mirror what is happening around them when they feel a relationship to whatever it is that is around them. For example, if you look at an old married couple, they are likely to constantly be mirroring each other's behaviors. It is essentially the ultimate culmination of empathy—the individuals are so bonded, so aware of each other and their behaviors, that they unconsciously mimic any behaviors that their partner does first. The two married people at the diner may both sip at their coffees at the same time as each other, or if one drinks, the other will follow shortly after. If one shifts in his seat, she will do so as well, always leaning to mirror the position her husband is in. If she brushes off something on her shoulder, he will unconsciously touch his shoulder as well. This act is known as mirroring, and it occurs in a wide range of circumstances.

You do not necessarily have to be a married couple that has been together for decades for mirroring to be relevant, either—you can see it everywhere. The person interviewing you for a job may begin to mirror you when the interview is going well, or the person who thinks that you are attractive may mimic some of your behaviors as well. You can see these behaviors mimicked started quite early on in terms of how long people have been interacting as well—sometimes people will even hit it off right off the bat and begin mirroring each other, emphasizing the fact that they seemed to have clicked.

Mirroring is essentially the ultimate form of flattery—it involves literally copying the other person because you like or love them so much. Children mirror their parents when learning how to behave in the world. Good friends often mirror each other. Salespeople wanting to win rapport, mirror people. No matter what the relationship is, if it is a positive one, there are likely mirroring behaviors, whether unconscious or not.

Uses of Mirroring

You may be wondering why something as simple as mimicry can actually be important to others, but it is actually one of the most fundamental parts of influence, persuasion, and manipulation. When you mirror someone, you can develop rapport. Rapport is essentially the measurement of your relationship with someone—if you have a good rapport with someone, you have developed some level of trust with them. The other person is likely to believe what you are saying if you develop rapport. However, if you have not yet developed rapport yet and you need the other person to listen to you, you can oftentimes artificially create that rapport through one simple task— mirroring. If you mirror the other person, you can essentially convince him to develop a rapport with you, whether it was something he wanted to develop on his own or whether you forced the point.

By constantly mirroring the other person, you essentially send the signs to their brain that they need to like this person because this person is just like them. Remember the three key factors for likability? The first one was able to relate or identify with the other person. In this case, you are presenting yourself as easy to relate to simply because you want the other person to like you. With liking you comes rapport. With rapport comes trust, which you can use to convince the other person to buy cars or do certain things that will benefit you. Building rapport even builds up the ability to be able to manipulate the other person—you need to be trustworthy for the other person to let you close enough to manipulate in the first place.

How to Mirror

Luckily for you, mirroring is quite easy to learn how to do. While it may seem awkward and unnatural at first, the more you practice it, the more natural it will become to you, and the more effective you can get at it. Remember, if you want to mirror someone, you will need to toe the line between too much and not enough. If you are too overt, the other person will catch on and will likely be more put off than convinced to like you. Take a look at these four steps so you can learn to mirror for yourself.

Build up a Connection

The first step when you are attempting to mirror someone is to start by building a connection somehow. If you do not feel the connection with the other person, they are not likely to be feeling a connection either. Keeping that in mind, you should begin to foster some sort of connection and rapport. This can be done with four simple steps on its own:

Fronting: This is the act of facing the other person entirely. You start with your body oriented toward them, directly facing the other person to give them your complete attention.

Eye contact: This is the tricky part—when you are making eye contact, you need to make sure that you get the right amount.

The triple nod: This does two things—it encourages the other person to keep speaking because the other person feels valued and listened to, and it makes the other person feel like you agree with them. It develops what is known as a yes set. The more you say yes, the more likely you are to develop a connection with the other person.

Fake it till you make it: At this point, you have spent a lot of time setting up the connection, and it is time for the moment of truth. You should imagine that the person is the most interesting in the world at that particular moment. You want to really believe that they are interesting to you. Then stop pretending—you should feel that they are actually interesting to you at this point. This is the birth of the connection you had been trying to establish.

Pace and Volume

Now, before you start mimicking their body language, start by paying attention to the other person's vocal cues. You want to make sure you are speaking at the same speed as the other person. If they are a quick speaker, you should also speak quickly, and if they are a slower speaker, you should slow your own speaking pace down to match. From there, make sure you are also mimicking the volume. If they are louder, you should raise your own voice. If they are keeping their voice down, you should follow suit. These vocal cues are far easier to mimic undetected than the rest of the physical cues.

The Punctuator

Everyone has a punctuator they use for emphasis. It could be something like a hand gesture that is used every time they want to emphasize something, or it could be the way they raise their brows as they say the word they want to stress. No matter what the punctuator is, you should identify what it is and seek to mimic it at the moment. Now, oftentimes, this cue is entirely unconscious on the other person's part, and as you begin to mimic it, the other person is likely to believe that you are on the same wavelength. This should really do it for you without making what you are doing obviously.

The Moment of Truth

Now, you are ready to test whether you have successfully built up the rapport you need. When you want to know if the other person has officially been connected to you, you should make some small action that is unrelated to what you are doing at that particular moment and see if the other person does it back. For example, if you are having a conversation about computers, you may reach up and rub your forehead for a split second. Watch and see if the other person also rubs at their forehead right after you. If they do, they have connected to you, and you can begin to move forward with your persuasive techniques.

Chapter 8:   Eye Reading

Reading eye contact is important to understand the true status of an individual, even where verbal communication seeks to hide it. As advised, body language should be read as a group, we will focus on individual aspects of body language and make the reader understand how to read that particular type of body language.

Your pupils dilate when you are focused and interested in someone you are having a conversation with, or the object we are looking at or using. The pupils will contract when one is transiting from one topic to another. We have no control over the working of pupils. When one is speaking about a less interesting topic, the pupils will contract.

Effective eye contact is critical when communicating with a person. Eye contact implies that one looks but does not stare. Persistent eye contact will make the recipient feel intimidated or judged. In Western cultures, regular eye contact is desired, but it should not be overly persistent. If one offers constant eye contact, then it is seen as an attempt to intimidate or judge, which makes the recipient of the eye contact uncomfortable. There are studies that suggest that most children fall victim to attacks by pet dogs if they make too much eye contact, as this causes them to feel threatened and react defensively and instinctually.

Winking

In Western culture, winking is considered as a form of flirting which should be done to people we are in good terms with. This varies, though, as Asian cultures frown on winking as a facial expression.

Blinking

In most cases, blinking is instinctive; our affection for the person we are speaking to causes us to subconsciously blink faster. If the average rate of blinking is 6 to 10 times per minute, then it can indicate that one is drawn to the person they are speaking to.

Eye Direction

The direction of the eyes tells us about how an individual is feeling. When someone is thinking, they tend to look to their left as they are recalling or reminiscing. An individual that is thinking tends to look to their right when thinking creatively, but it can also be interpreted as a sign that one is lying. For left-handed people, the eye directions will be reversed.

Avoiding Eye Contact

When we do not make eye contact with someone we are speaking to for extended periods of time, we are most likely uncomfortable with the person or the conversation. We avoid looking someone in the eye if we feel ashamed to be communicating at them. When we feel dishonest about trying to deceive people, we avoid looking at them. While it is okay to blink or drop eye contact temporarily, people that consistently shun making eye contact are likely to be feeling uneasy with the message or the person they are communicating with. For emphasis, staring at someone will make them drop eye contact due to feeling intimidated. Evasive eye contact happens where one deliberately avoids making eye contact.

Crying

Human beings cry due to feeling uncontrollable pain or in an attempt to attract sympathy from others. Crying is considered an intense emotion associated with grief or sadness though it can also denote extreme happiness known as tears of joy. When an individual force tears to manipulate a situation, this is referred to as "crocodile tears." Typically, though, if one cries, then the individual is likely experiencing intense negative emotion.

Additionally, when one is interested in what you are speaking, he or she will make eye contact often. The eye contact on the eyes of the other person is for the duration of 2-3 minutes, and then it switches to the lips or nose, and then returns to the eyes. For a brief moment, the person initiating eye contact will look down then back up to the eyes. Looking up and to the right demonstrates dismissal and boredom. Dilation of the pupil may indicate that someone is interested or that the room is brighter.

In some instances, sustained eye contact may be a signal that you want to speak to the person or that you are interested in the person sexually. At one point, you have noticed a hard stare from a man towards a particular woman to the point the woman notices and asks the man what is all that for. In this case, eye contact is not being used to intimidate but to single out the target person. You probably have seen a woman ask why is that man staring at me then she proceeds to mind her business but on taking another look at the direction of the man the stare is still there. In this manner, eye contact is used to single out an individual and make them aware that one is having sexual feelings towards the person.

However, people are aware of the impact of body language and will seek to portray the expected body language. For instance, an individual that is lying is likely to make deliberate eye contact frequently to sound believable. At one point, you knew you were lying but went ahead to make eye contact. You probably have watched movies where one of the spouses is lying but makes believable eye contact with others. The reason for this faked body language is because the person is aware of the link between making eye contact and speaking the truth.

Like verbal language, body language and in particular eye contact can be highly contextual. For instance, an individual may wink to indicate that he or she agrees with the quality of the product being presented or that he or she agrees with the plan. Eye contact in these settings can be used as a coded language for a group of people. At one point, one of your classmates may have used a wink to indicate that the teacher is coming or to indicate that the secret you have been guarding is now out.

The Definite, Firm, Open View

Many people believe that a definite, fixed gaze should go hand in hand with an immobile pupil, as opposed to the restless gaze. But that's not true, because a fixed view is always an unsteady one. Think about it: If you remember the last time you looked really hard into someone's eyes, you looked that person in the eyes, not in the eye. That is, your gaze kept moving from one eye to the other. If your last such experience was so long ago that you cannot imagine this process at the moment, go to the mirror and try eye contact with yourself.

Do you have a clear picture of this process in your mind's eye? Then you understand that a firm look must be a moving one! If one were to really see someone else firmly in the eye (i.e. to fix him), then the feeling that was triggered by it would be a most alienating one.

Therefore, it is not surprising that one feels uncomfortable in the presence of some people who have learned and trained eye contact in an exaggerated form. If you for example, if you have the opportunity to speak with members of the Church of Scientology (also known as Dianetics), which is also in Germany, then you can watch this constant stare. If this is then accompanied by a frozen light smile, as "masters" of the system understand it to radiate, then the impression of having to deal with a robotic-programmed, depersonalized person becomes even stronger. Similar observations can also be made with American graduates of several EST courses, as well as with the followers of many juvenile sects, also with participants of some so-called rhetoric seminars!

Eye Contact

Eye contact is called eye contact because it creates contact.

Now, eye contact can also avoid this contact, although he seems to be looking for him. This is the case when one stares at someone. A rule of some rhetoric and communication coach states. For example, one should see the other firmly and definitely on the root of the nose. This cannot promote genuine, warm, understanding contact, but must be strange! In addition, the pupil movements when stared at a spot are so minimal that they can hardly be perceived by the naked eye. While a lively look, in which one wanders from pupil to pupil, is the kind of gaze we mean by eye contact.

Now the theory says that the eye is an excellent indicator of interest. But please do not forget that it can only be an indicator because also the chest cavity, as well as the mouth, play an essential role here.

In eye contact, we can, therefore, assume that the communication is good. But what about when eye contact is avoided? First an experiment again: Have a conversation with someone in the near future, in which you will tell each other something. If you could quickly chat with a neighbor or colleague before you read on, it would be optimal. They will pay attention to eye contact and try to determine what good eye contact is.

If you have an opportunity to try this, you will notice the following statement:

Contrary to popular belief, good eye contact is not constant. Instead, we understand by good eye contact that the listener (almost) constantly looks at the, while the speaker looks at the listener less frequently. This is related to the fact that we cannot simultaneously think intensely and perceive information that is irrelevant to this process of thought. Therefore, a reflection often looks up at the ceiling (as if it were written there) or sideways away or down. This look is not really a look, because he is not consciously aware right now. He looks inward, or sinks in thought.

The more someone has to think or want what he wants to say, the more likely he is to interrupt eye contact. You can also test this again specifically.

Chapter 9:   Ways Your Body Language Can Project Confidence

Mastering the art of reading and analyzing people has some great benefits. It helps you protect yourself against harm, it keeps you in control of your interactions with others, and it also does something incredible for you. It makes you a highly effective communicator. You are able to build rapport, resolve conflicts, and nurture the relationships that matter to you. In short, it makes you become a better version of yourself. What many of us don't realize when we pick up material like this to educate ourselves on how to read others is that by doing that, we also learn to understand ourselves better. We discover ways of becoming more of the individual we have always wanted to be. You can continue to improve yourself and become who you were meant to be, keep in remind that one of the main identifiers that we all subconsciously use to determine how highly we rate someone for the first time - the handshake. As soon as you meet someone for the first time, they will read and make a judgment of you based on your outward appearance, facial expression, and most definitely based on your handshake. So, in case you are still unsure about what handshake to develop moving forward, let's devote a little time to that now.

The Best Kind of Handshake

There are a lot of Do's and Don'ts when it comes to handshakes, and if you remember, I wrote a whole segment on the types of handshakes that are considered awful. Read them once again and make sure you steer clear of them. Instead, what I want to focus on here is the best handshake you can start practicing.

The best handshake that will communicate the right message to the person in front of you involves the palms of both you and the other person positioned vertically. Practice some self-awareness here, and if you realize the presser you are applying is greater or much lesser than the other person, then regulate yourself quickly. Don't offer a submissive or a dominating handshake. Submissive is when your palm is facing up and falls below the palm of the other person. In so doing, you're giving the other person the upper hand. Dominant is the opposite of submissive and indicates to the other person that you want to dominate.

Use the double handler instead. It is considered one of the most potent handshakes in the world. To do it right, you need both hands. First, the person presents you with a palm down thrust, and then you step in and respond with a palm up and apply your second hand to make the palm of the other person straight. Use this handshake, and you will always display the right amount of equality in power and subconsciously send the right message to the other person.

Does Mirroring Work?

We have been using mirror techniques since infancy. Yes, mirroring is a powerful technique, and many of us already do it to some degree, especially with people we are closely connected to.

Mirroring with strangers also works if you do it naturally and with the right rhythm. Done poorly, you just come across looking like a creep. However, when you learn to read the body cues others are sending and use them in subtle ways to mirror back to them what you feel they are experiencing, it is a great way to establish a sense of bond. People will feel like you get them. What this comes down to (assuming you want to do it appropriately) is to practice as much as you can by doing it in a way that feels and seems natural to you. If you imitate or mimic for the sake of being like the other person, it will backfire on you.

7 Effective Ways to Show Your Confidence

Many studies show that people who appear more confident tend to achieve more success in life. If you want to become who you were meant to be in life, increasing your level of confidence is a must. You can only successfully apply all the knowledge if you've got sufficient amounts of confidence; otherwise, you'll continuously doubt yourself, overexert your efforts and end up passing the wrong body language to the people you interact with. Here are seven practical ways you can increase and show that you're a confident person.

1. Stand up straight with your spine erect, head level, and shoulders relaxed. Good posture is vital to appear confident. People who slouch or carry a misaligned body posture struggle to communicate that they are confident. Make sure you're posture is aligned correctly.

2. Maintain the right amount of direct eye contact. You don't want your eyes wandering across the room, and you also don't want to stare too long at someone without blinking. Find a perfect cadence with your eye movement that works for you. What you want to aim for is a rapport, almost like a shared dance between you and the person you are addressing.

3. Avoid fidgeting, and definitely do not tap your feet. There are certain habits we develop over time, such as tapping our feet on the ground (something I've been guilty of), jingling coins in the pocket, twirling the hair (ladies), or too much swaying back and forth. These habits, while harmless, can make you come across as lacking confidence. They also distract the person listening to you and thereby dilute the message you're attempting to communicate.

4. Avoid placing your hands in your pocket or jacket. Your hands should be visible when addressing someone. Whenever you pocket your hands, it sends off the signal that you're nervous, uncomfortable, and uncertain. To come across as confident, make sure your hands are visible, and your palms face up as much as possible.

5. Find your strong and powerful voice. The best way to speak in a tone, pitch, and cadence that comes across as powerful and strong is to talk while pressing down firmly on your abdominal muscles. In other words, you want to draw your power from your stomach area. That will ensure it carries more emotional conviction and also lowers the pitch a bit, which makes you project strength. It will take a bit of practice, but the more you do it, the more you will tell the difference between your weak voice and your strong voice.

6. Carry a positive open body posture and make an effort to be interested instead of impressive. If you want to show confidence, engage with the person in front of you. Immerse yourself in the present moment instead of worrying about yourself, how you look, what you'll say next etc. The more focus you place on the other person, the more they will perceive you as being confident and interesting.

7. Avoid using filler words. I think this is pretty straightforward. The fewer the filler words you use, such as

"um," "like," "uh," and "so," the better. You will come across as more concise and clearer in your communication, which will project confidence. I also encourage you to take the time to pronounce your words clearly. People who speak too fast or run through their words often sound nervous and less confident. Be comfortable to address people at a tempo that helps you fully express yourself.

When it comes to showing confidence, there is no magic pill to swallow or shortcut you can take. It comes down to how willing you are to work on yourself daily, improve the aspects of yourself that still need improving, and boldly share with the world your authentic expression. The more you can discover who you really are and authentically share that with the world unapologetically, the easier it will be to convey confidence.

Chapter 10:   Body Language and Seduction

Being able to detect if a person is truly into you can save a lot of time and heartache when dating. There are specific body movements that are unique to men and women that display attraction. Sure, words are incredible, but actions are momentous. This form of body language is the most sensual in nature and inviting. Many of the common depictions on cartoons and illustrations are quite accurate when it comes to flirting. Women have a unique set of body language cues that are attractive to men. It complements their feminine role and can be used as a form of luring the man in. Men demonstrate a similar display of body cues that align with their masculinity. Oftentimes, the cues are so strong, they release certain hormones related to sexual attraction. The act of engaging in sexual pleasure is body language at its height. Since words are not commonly used as a sexual act, intercourse is the purest form of visually displaying that attraction. Let's consider the primary difference between men and women when it comes to displaying attraction.

Women

When a woman finds a male attractive, she may begin by locking eyes with him. She could give a subtle gaze and then look away. If this continues, the woman essentially wants the man to chase her. Simple touches to the body and even her curling her hair with fingers are used to flirt. This brings attention to the feminine qualities of a woman that may be attractive to the man. When a woman raises her eyebrows when talking with a man, they are signaling attraction. She may see the man as genuinely attractive or admirable. Or she may be so caught up in what he is saying that it moves her to agree. The lips also show fascination, particularly in the biting, licking, or touching them. At the point when a lady looks intently at a man's lips and makes direct contact, this is a subconscious invitation to kiss.

As mentioned previously, women tend to lean in toward their dates to show attraction. When her legs are crossed inward, facing her date, it's a suggestive pose that indicates sexual interest. This is elevated when the privates are exposed and involved a light caress. Ladies may also curve their backs to extend their spines additionally. The arch of their spine is a female quality that is alluring to the man. Slight presentation of the bosom is an indication of an exceptional tease. She is bringing the man into her womanhood to express interest.

Women may also "bat" their eyes up and down rapidly as a sign of flirtation. This brings attention to the lashes which, when elongated, are physically pleasing to the man. She may pair this with a slight giggle to signal attraction.

Oftentimes, women tend to "mirror" the movements of men. This signifies submission as the woman is showing respect for the position of the man. Inadvertently, she is following the lead of her date. Many sensual dances rely on the man leading and the woman following. Women subconsciously perform these acts as a means to show respect for the men's masculinity.

Men

When a man moves his head slightly, raises his eyebrows, and permits his nostrils to flare, he is indicating fascination. When paired with a smile, the level of attraction is heightened. Initially, a man will avoid making direct eye contact as he may be nervous or unaware of the woman's attraction level. In addition, men speak with their chest. If the chest is pointing towards the woman, he is giving her his full attention. If his chest is pointing elsewhere, he secretly wants to escape the situation.

Men want to appear dominant, masculine, and strong to perspective dates. They may stand with their feet wide and their hands on their hips in order to appear sturdy. If his hands are gracing his waist line, he essentially wants the woman to look near his genitals. This is a silent invitation to a possible sexual encounter. Men tend to show their attraction through their hands. Slight touches to the back, thigh, and arm indicates sexual attraction. However, a pat on the shoulder could be read as platonic.

There are universal indications of fascination completed by men and women. Grinning and a willingness to laugh without fear are significant signs. Spatial awareness is a key indicator to revealing intent. When two people are attracted to each other, they tend to stand close. Their shoulders are raised and positioned inwardly which indicates interest. Even the positioning of the toes symbolizes attraction. As mentioned, the toes point to where they want to go. When the toes are facing each other, sometimes called "pigeon toed," they are subtle signs of flirting. The man or woman wants to appear cute and coy. This vulnerable position subconsciously boosts sexual attraction. The palms traditionally reveal truth. When a man or a woman is interested, their palms may rest in an exposed position. It promotes openness which indicates that the two would like to get to know each other.

The laws of attraction are traditional as they signify small psychological changes that are quite universal. When a person speaks their intent with body language cues to follow, you can guarantee their validity. By understanding these simple cues, you will be better equipped to make accurate perceptions about the intent of others.

Chapter 11:   Body Language and Work

Body Language in Business

Nonverbal communication plays a very important role in business negotiations and meetings.

There are different movements of the body, many of them unconscious which transmit nerves, fear, insecurity, etc. And while you are in a meeting with an important client or in the middle of a negotiation with a possible strategic ally is totally inconvenient your body is sending the wrong signs.

We will share body language which will help you to be secure, confident and determinate when doing business:

- Rest your arm on the adjacent chair whenever possible; claiming more space you are showing more power, but don't lose the straight posture of your back.

- Touching your throat while speaking will make you nervous and insecure; placing your hand under your chin you project self-confidence.

- When you keep your ankles crossed demonstrates discomfort and isolation keeping them parallel denotes confidence.

- Placing a hand over the classic handshake is considered very aggressive in business, if someone does it with you, take the other person by the forearm to regain your power.

- When the handshake tends to be horizontal the person with the hand up is exercising power while the other is being submissive. Make sure your handshake is firm and with only one hand.

- During the greeting it is essential to maintain eye contact unless you want take the risk of looking absolutely disinterested in the other person.

- Placing your hands on your waist momentarily will make you see and even feel confident about yourself.

The gesture of crossing our arms over the chest can project us as persons who close ourselves to others, it can also express that we are considering an idea.

Oscillating and allowing our gaze to be easily distracted is not a good sign for our interlocutor. We demonstrate we don't care about what he is saying.

Studying the customs of each country is essential. For instance, in the West, receiving a business card with one hand is something common. In Japan it's mandatory to receive it with both hands.

In the same way the OK emblem we make by touching and cupping the tips of the thumb and index finger, means you have zero power, you are extremely insignificant in Europe, while in

Brazil it is considered a vulgar gesture and the thumb up gesture that for Westerners means "Everything is fine" in Saudi Arabia is the equivalent of giving the finger to someone.

Power Postures Which Project Leadership

Leadership and body language. How are they related? This is a phrase that is repeated a lot "For others to see you as a leader, you have to act as if you believed it yourself". And it's true. At least, that's what experts on the subject say. It is not enough to have certain capacities or leadership qualities to become one, it is also necessary to know how to project that figure to others, especially when we interact with our employees. And for this, there are different leadership and body language guidelines that can be learned and can help you to achieve it.

Keys to Communicate with Your Team:

1. First of all, you need to project a trustworthy image. Be careful with your postures and movements, because they say a lot about you. When communicating with our team or employees, it is best to adopt a posture as natural as possible, which favors a pleasant atmosphere and conversation. Pay special attention to your feet and legs, don't move them excessively, don't open your legs too far or put your hands in your pockets. Actually, the less you move them, the better. According to Carol Goman (body language expert), reducing your movements can make you gain authority. You have to offer an image of self-confidence, calm and security, so you have to keep a deep and constant breath, with controlled movements.

2. Your face says a lot too. Gestures should not be forgotten, of course. Just as body movement can express our nervousness or calm, our face will be the most important focus of attention. Experts recommend paying special attention to our gaze, which must express confidence and decision. It is always important to look into the eyes of our interlocutor, to hold the gaze, because this way we will impact the person we have in front of us. This denotes security and confidence in yourself and in the message, you want to communicate.

3. A tone of voice appropriate for the message. The voice is another of the elements through which we communicate and that reflects our mood and personality. When addressing our team, a low tone in our voice can denote insecurity, reflected in our words and even fear. A tone too high can be perceived as an excessive authority. The ideal in a conversation with the team or negotiation is to vary the tone of your voice as the conversation develops, raising the tone to emphasize some aspects. A good tip is also to give your words more precision by separating some syllables and pointing the finger in order to give more strength to the message. Something quite common in politicians, for instance.

4. Straight but relaxed. Maintain a straight posture, with your back straight and your head high (which will also allow you to see yourself a few inches higher), but without looking too arrogant. Try to offer a relaxed image. While walking, try to offer security, confidence and also command with each step.

5. Answering questions is quite a science. As body language experts recommend, avoid taking too long to answer a question, as it will denote insecurity. Nor do we must

project the sense of choosing the right words to give our interlocutor what he or she wants to hear. As far as possible, expressions of the type "Ahhhh", "Mmmm", which may transmit nervousness and even insecurity in our message, must be avoided. Before answering, experts also recommend to look straight, and avoiding looking to one side or low the eyes, since these gestures can be interpreted as shyness or lack of confidence.

Women and Leadership

Body language in men and women presents very different behaviors, generated after centuries of imposition regarding certain educational and cultural guidelines. Both have advantages and disadvantages, but signs of power and leadership are associated, in part, with masculine gestures mainly. Therefore, women managers must learn new nonverbal habits which allow them to claim authority with the body as well.

Women occupy only one in four of managerial positions worldwide, despite representing almost half of the population, according to recent studies. However, as evidenced by Jack Zenger and Joe Folkman's research in collaboration with the Harvard Business Review, female leaders scored better than their male counterparts in 12 of the 16 competencies, which currently conform the extraordinary leadership.

Actually, the main strength of female managers is, as a general rule, empathy, a positive characteristic that can become a handicap in some scenarios. It's also perceived as a sign for lacking of authority or submission. Therefore, the body language of women leaders is very important in order to curb that image of weakness.

Body Language in Female Leadership

There are two types of signs in body language regarding leadership: the person's warmth, and on the other hand, the authority. In the case of the female group, the first factor is common and well known, while demonstrating the second is quite difficult. Women must take advantage of body language movements to be projected as powerful and self-confident leaders.

Head Tilts. In body language, tilting the head denotes interest and concern towards the sender, but is also associated as a symbol of submission. For this reason, this gesture –particularly feminine- should be limited to those situations in which you want to demonstrate that active listening of the interlocutor, while the head must maintain a more neutral position when you want to demonstrate power.

Body space. Authority, at the level of nonverbal communication, is linked to height and space. For instance, at first sight, a small person is perceived as less powerful than an average height one. Consequently, women must learn to cover more space with their bodies, stretching their shoulders, separating the arms from the body, or spreading their belongings on the meeting table, instead of making a neat pile next to them.

Children's Gestures. In stressful situations, boys rub their hands or touch their necks and faces, but women twist strands of hair or play with the necklace or ring, giving the image of a little girl. To show more power, women leaders need to forget these gestures and choose to keep their hands still in their lap or on the table.

Declarative Tone. When women make an affirmation, they usually end the sentences with a high tone, as if asking or seeking approval, which is an indication of submission. The solution is to make sure that the tonal arc of the statement begins on a note, increases through the sentence, and descends at the end, rather than rising.

Smile. Women smile more than men as a way to please and, although the smile is a great ally when it comes to empathizing with others, overused, it can become a credibility thief, especially in situations where there is some tension.

Assent. The men agree to let their interlocutor know that they agree, but the women use this gesture continuously: to say that they share the idea, that they understand it, they want the other person to continue... It is just another example of this cultural need of the woman for being accepted. However, it's the same case when they tilt their head; to project authority, you have to keep your head still.

Interruptions. In a meeting of women and men, men are more likely to intervene more frequently and continually interrupt their partners. For this reason, the author advises women managers not to be afraid to raise their voices, to be heard without wait for men to give them the floor.

Flirtation. Some women flirt as a weapon to achieve their ends. However, a study from the University of Berkeley showed that people preferred those professionals who were correct and competent in their body language over those who tried to flirt during a sale.

Emotions. The female group has less ability to control emotions and is usually excessively expressive in their behavior. If the objective is to motivate or involve, this passion can be positive, but it is convenient to avoid it when you want to give an image of authority.

Handshake. Women who shake hands softly are viewed as passive and insecure. A firm squeeze, coupled with a look into the other person's eyes, is a simple change in body language which will help to improve the perception of a woman manager.

Chapter 12: Effective Body Language in Job Interview

Did you know that giving every interviewer a strong resume or curriculum vitae nowadays does not necessarily guarantee you are landing the job? You might also be able to correctly answer all the focused questions; however, if the body language sends the wrong signals and messages throughout the interview, you will still not be close to receiving and signing the letter of appointment.

It may come as no surprise for many, but statistical data have also shown words have only succeeded in contributing 35% of the message being transmitted, while the tone of your voice and body language has a command of 65% of what is communicated.

Whether you're a confident person or not, whether you're the open and friendly guy or the shy and quiet man, whether you're a team player or a solo loner, or whether or not you're honest and genuine. The interviewer will not only pay attention to what you say during the question-and-answer phase but will also analyze carefully the way you say it. You will then look for all those comments, reactions, and answers from you that suit their requirements for the offered role.

If or not you put it in your mouth, body language will show your true feelings to the interviewer. If you are without the knowledge or awareness of your negative attributes from your actions, you definitely won't be able to get on their right side. Signals and movements such as anxiety, fear, weariness, dullness, dishonesty, and lack of integrity can potentially project your bad image and lose you the job application.

It is difficult to overemphasize the significance of body language during the first four or five minutes of the encounter. A bright and enduring impression will be created within this short period that can dramatically affect the outcome of the meeting. Please wait for the interviewer to raise his or her hand first as a sign of respect and politeness before offering yours for the handshake. Grip and shake the hand tightly while holding eye contact, but do not squeeze. Primarily, a robust optimistic handshake produces the best results for encouraging confidence. In comparison, soft and awkward handshakes will only transmit a half-hearted message that will only undermine and degrade an otherwise optimistic situation.

Start seated only after the interviewer has told you to do so. At the same time, be aware of your surroundings and stop having to face a bright and shiny window, as this will make it difficult for you to maintain good eye contact. Try not to be afraid to ask or demand politically for a seat change if you have no opportunity or preference to stop the sunlight glare.

You will need to put yourself in a positive and relaxed way to start in the right direction and altogether avoid projecting any negative patterns in body language. Make sure you always have space for yourself to shift and reposition if you happen to be restless or rigid.

Raise your head to the same eye level as the interviewer to display an engaging smile, while at the same time relaxing your back, but not to the point of slumping to the floor. Place your hands on your lap loosely or place them on your chair's armrest. By doing so, you can use hand movements at any moment to help what you say to clarify your comments and make the conversation more interesting. The interviewer will look at you as confident and comfortable with the progress of the interview with hand gestures that support your words. Bear in mind not to get too excited and result in overdoing in excess the gestures and actions, as this will project only an uncomfortable shape that indicates anxiety or hostility.

All the Essential and Useful Body Language Movements and Signs You Must Always Be Mindful During Interviews

- Using Your Voice Power Successfully, express confidence and excitement through your voice's firmness.

- Don't pinch too hard on your face. High-pitch voices are heard over the years, making you sound like a whining child.

- Avoid enthusiastic gabbling and mumbling because no one trusts a speedy speaker.

- Vary the conversation voice and dynamics, so avoid talking too loudly or too softly.

- Talk slightly slower than usual to keep your presence smooth and steady, but don't overdo it.

- Always pause to avoid unconsciously responding and having the wrong words coming out of your mouth before beginning the next word.

- Test your tone range to prevent dreary and weary monotonous speech.

Negative Body Language Behavior and Habits to Avoid

- A fixed or distracted look indicates that either you're dreaming during the day or your mind is somewhere else.

- Hesitating or looking away before or during your speaking time indicates you're unsure about what you're doing.

- Constantly rubbing your eyes or mouth while talking means you're deceptive or hiding something.

- Doodling on paper shows that you don't pay attention and that you don't care.

- It's irritating, distracting, and a sure sign of boredom to click your foot continuously.

- Arms folded or crossed suggest a refusal and a reluctance to listen.

- Constant fidgeting suggests frustration and restlessness.

Favorable Postures and Gestures

- Attentive: nodding, grinning

- Listening: verbal recognition, nodding, tilting of the head, constant eye contact

- Responsive: open arms, leaning back, nodding negative postures and gestures

- Lying/deception: glancing around, rubbing of the ears, averting of the eyes, hands over the mouth, awkward shifting of the chair

- Aggression: clenched fists, cutting hands.

- Don't fidget when you feel uncomfortable when you're sitting. Slightly change your position and sit up straight to keep an alert.

- If you are faced with a difficult question, stay calm before answering and be aware of your negative body language patterns. Stop jumping into an unpredictable expression.

- Watch and mimic the movements of the interviewer. When laughing, laughing with them, leaning forward to illustrate an argument, lean forward to demonstrate your attention. Postural and gestural echoes bring together, and you will receive a more precise answer.

- Relax to create a relaxed and comfortable look. Do not hurry through the interview; simply flow the pace and let the interviewer set the pace.

- Keep eye contact consistent and alert, but try to stop looking from time to time.

- Smile expression can give positive emotional reactions. It will restore your enjoyable nature and enthusiasm, but be mindful of senselessly over-delivering.

At job interviews, body posture and movement are vital ingredients. Through our facial expressions, the sound of our voice, and also our eye language, our emotions, and inner feelings are easily conveyed to the interviewer. Make sure that you always sound relaxed and optimistic by speaking with a calm, consistent, and managed voice that can be easily heard and understood. Thin and soft voices do not seem to have the vital energy and do not inspire faith in others.

What you want to do here is to focus and use your body language to define your abilities, qualities, and values to maximize the interviewer's potential.

Take some time before the actual interview day to practice and rehearse using the role-play technique with a family member or a relative. Note that it makes training better. You will protect half of the job before you even enter the room when you are well trained.

One final thing you always have to consider, as this is the most critical aspect of any job interview. Be on time and arrive on time. Being late is to say goodbye to the conversation more or less before it even has an opportunity to start. There will be no company interested in employing a person lacking in professionalism and corporate ethics. Being early by an hour is much better than being late by just one minute.

Chapter 13: Powerful Body Language in Public Speaking

Making an excellent introduction includes more than thinking of a subject or planning the ideal PowerPoint to go with it. While those things are significant, there is one more excellent component that you have to focus on—your body language.

While the introduction format you use is significant, your body language during an introduction can have a significant effect between a fruitful introduction and an absolute catastrophe.

Along these lines, you shouldn't think little of the significance of body language in introductions, and right now, clarify what body language is alongside various sorts of body language and offer amazing body language tips that you can use for your next introduction.

Body language is how your body imparts without the utilization of words. It consolidates hand gestures, posture, outward appearances, and developments that mention to others what's happening inside your head. Body language can happen intentionally and unwittingly.

For instance, how you're sitting right currently, combined with your outward appearance, can educate others a great deal concerning you. Given your body language, they can tell whether you're diverted or thinking hard. They can determine whether you're congenial or in case you're having a terrible day.

In case you're in a conversation with somebody and verbally concur with them, your body language will either affirm that you, to sure agree with what is being said, or deceive you and tell others you don't feel a similar way.

Your body language uncovers the real story behind your words.

The Impact of Body Language in Effective Presentations

Utilizing body language in introductions the correct way can assist you with bringing more deals to a close or win that pitch. Your body language can assist you with drawing in your crowd and be sure and loose during your introduction. At the point when you look, keep up a sure posture and eye contact, your introduction will be progressively powerful, and you'll have the option to associate with your crowd.

Despite what might be expected, on the off chance that you don't focus on it, terrible body language during an introduction, for example, slumping, no eye contact or arms on hips will cause your introduction to seem dull, and you'll end up estranging your crowd.

The Body Language Tips for A Professional Public Speaking

Since we've secured what body language is and why it makes a difference while giving an introduction, here are ten hints that will tell you the best way to utilize body language to improve your introduction.

Grin

In all honesty, a grin is the most useful asset you have in your body language tool kit. Grinning can be as invigorating as getting as much as 16,000 Pounds Sterling in real money." What's progressive, a grin can right away change the observation we have about somebody. Also, it drives individuals to grin back at us.

While the facts confirm that grinning can be hard when you're anxious, however, remember that a University of Kansas study found that grinning lessens the pressure. In this way, whenever you're up there giving an introduction, remember to grin from time to time. Not exclusively will you appear to be increasingly agreeable to your crowd, yet you'll calm that pressure you're feeling too.

Try not to Slouch

Slumping causes you to show up less sure and like you're conveying the heaviness of the world on your shoulders. On the off chance that you're genuinely ready to stand straight, at that point, make certain to do so whenever you're giving an introduction. Stand tall and straight with your shoulders pulled back and your stomach took care of—you'll show up progressively certain and get a speedy shock of vitality for sure.

Expect a Power Pose

Force posture can assist you in setting up power when you have to seem to be certain and definitive in your introduction. A case of a force present is remaining with your feet a shoulder-width separated, with hands-on your hips, and jaw lifted up. In any case, be mindful so as not to try too hard, except if you need to put on a show of being threatening. Save the force models for essential pieces of your introduction.

Utilize the Space

Another snappy tip is to utilize the stage. Rather than stopping, move around the stage. Thusly, you'll make an impression on your crowd that you're agreeable in your skin and sure about your point matter. It'll additionally assist you with abstaining from squirming.

Venture out from behind the platform and let your crowd see you. Start from one spot then onto the next by making a few strides, halting, and afterward making a couple of more strides.

Be normal as you move about, however, and abstain from pacing as this will accomplish the contrary impact and make you look apprehensive. Also, you'll come up short on breath.

Remember Facial Expressions

Outward appearances can do for keeping your crowd intrigued and persuading them to have faith in your motivation. Your introduction isn't the time nor the spot to expedite your poker face as you'll put on a show of being a robot.

By letting your enthusiasm for your point radiate through with your outward appearances, your crowd will have the option to interface with you and trust you. An expression of alert, however: don't deliberately go over the edge with your outward appearances as this will put on a show of being misrepresenting and undependable.

You can rehearse your outward appearances before the mirror while you practice your discourse. On the other hand, record yourself with a camera and investigate your outward appearances later on.

Speak Clearly

It's normal for the nerves to show signs of improvement of you during the introduction, and you falter or mutter, particularly if there are precarious words included. Rehearsing your discourse before the introduction is a decent method to ensure you feel great conveying it and that your crowd will have the option to get you.

Another tip that will assist you with talking obviously and unquestionably is to envision you're conveying your introduction to your companions.

Try Not to Be Afraid to Gesture

In the event that you watch different moderators, you'll notice one thing in like manner: every single extraordinary moderator consistently uses hand gestures to help convey their introduction. Hand gestures will enable you to push what's significant, just as express sentiments and feelings. Your enthusiasm for the subject will turn out to be increasingly clear as our gestures are all the more exuberant when we're enthusiastic about something.

Hand gestures will show your crowd you care about the introduction subject and that you're a successful communicator, so don't be hesitant to utilize them during an introduction.

Keep in touch

As you give your introduction, make certain to keep in touch with your crowd and face them. Doing so will cause them to feel like you're talking legitimately to them and will help keep them inspired by your introduction.

Staying away from eye contact or turning your back to them, then again, will put on a show of being discourteous and break the association with the crowd.

Make Sure to Breathe

While you're on the stage, it very well may be very simple to become involved with your introduction and begin to talk quickly. However, in the event that you talk excessively quickly, your crowd will block out in light of the fact that it'll be difficult to tail you, and you'll come up short on breath. That is the reason it's essential to take a respite and make sure to relax. Breathing appropriately will likewise assist you with your voice pitch and tone, so you don't sound stressed and anxious.

Gain from Other Presenters

The last tip is to gain from other extraordinary moderators. You can examine their body language and perceive how they utilize outward appearances, development, and gestures to assist them with passing on their thoughts.

Chapter 14: Neuro-Linguistic Programming (NLP) Non-Verbal Communication

To make companions and impact individuals utilizing NLP non-verbal communication is from one perspective unquestionably do-capable yet then again would require some examination and practice so as to get gifted and compelling with it. The craftsmanship and study of non-verbal communication use and the translation isn't some unpredictable and arcane control yet involves having a careful comprehension of it and furthermore the development of a specific nuance of the brain.

NLP non-verbal communication is fundamentally about making compatibility with the other individual or, in the event that you were an exceptionally talented professional, gathering of people. Making and building affinity utilizing non-verbal correspondence to support your verbal correspondence relies upon one key factor, that being valid.

This identifies with the procedure of "reflecting", otherwise known as "coordinating" or "process pacing". Reflecting depends on what is really a straightforward mental establishment, that being that two individuals who are managing everything well together once in a while will in general unpretentiously mirror or match each other's signals and developments. In no legitimately clear method for a course - that is the place credibility comes into it - however, in unpretentious manners that wouldn't regularly be seen by the cognizant brain yet would be by the intuitive.

What's more, it's your subliminal brain that at last chooses for you whether you like, trust or are pulled in to somebody. You'll in all likelihood sooner in your grown-up life have asked why somebody you just met caused you to feel quiet or uncomfortable by and large. That individual's unpretentious non-verbal communication which you subliminally got on very quickly had a great deal to do with that.

As to the way toward utilizing reflecting methods to assemble affinity, there is any way a sort of chicken and egg factor around this. Individuals who manage everything well together in some cases unwittingly reflect each other's emotions and peculiarities, however, that happens on the grounds that the compatibility as of now exists, the affinity itself isn't really made by the reflecting.

So consequently in the event that you need to utilize NLP related non-verbal communication systems, for example, reflecting or coordinating so as to help make and fabricate compatibility with somebody, for instance, somebody who is talking with you as a potential activity competitor or somebody, you discover alluring or somebody you need to settle a negotiations with, at that point, you must be mindful so as to utilize reflecting inconspicuously and sparingly.

NLP Body Language Signs

Validness would by and large be considerably more effectively and viably accomplished by somebody with positive expectations. This means somebody who was utilizing reflecting systems so as to help make a really adjusted, commonly aware and useful relationship would in general be considerably more fruitful at utilizing reflecting than would somebody who was utilizing it for negative reasons, for example, a longing to control and apply power/control.

Contrarily propelled reflecting will, in general, be to some degree ungainly and effectively observed through and in this manner insufficient. On the off chance that no certifiable affinity exists in any case and you, at that point attempt to reflect somebody's quirks so as to impact them, they will more likely than not get on the endeavored trickery intuitively and conceivably intentionally.

Be that as it may, if your aims are sure, in that you need that activity since you realize you'd be acceptable at it, or you need to finalize that negotiations since you realize that it's a decent arrangement for all, or you need to get along with that individual you find alluring on the grounds that you feel that you would be extraordinary together, at that point a specific measure of compatibility is as of now there. Reflecting strategies would then be able to be utilized, inconspicuously and sparingly, to expand on and fortify that affinity.

A portion of the more typical motions and characteristics noted in NLP non-verbal communication contemplates incorporate seating positions, intersection and uncrossing of legs or lower legs, inclining forward to confront one another, hand developments or motions, for example, hand on the jaw as though considering something or fastening and unclasping of hands. Furthermore, obviously grinning - truly - at one another is generally perceived just like a compelling affinity manufacturer.

There are obviously incalculable different quirks that can be reflected. The most ideal approach to begin learning this expertise is to glance around and watch people groups' peculiarities and signals out in the open places, for example, bars and eateries and so forth.

One of the principle "rules" identifying with the reflecting procedure includes permitting a brief pause before coordinating a specific motion or development that somebody has made. In the event that, for instance, you're sitting with somebody confronting each other over a table and the other individual sooner during the discussion fastens their hands together on the table, stick around 20 seconds before coordinating the signal, regardless of whether inside that time the individual has unclasped their hands once more.

The other individual will have intuitively noticed this, and, if it's done quietly and legitimately and has been one of a few motions and peculiarities that you have inconspicuously and truly reflected over the span of the discussion, this will all tend to "feed" the other individual's subliminal with the impression and feeling that you are on a similar wavelength as them, that you're both "in agreement" together, that your emotions, perspectives, and interests are by one way or another conjoined.

Remember however that NLP non-verbal communication coordinating ought to never be utilized unnecessarily or thought of (by awkward masterminds) as the most important thing in the world of making compatibility. In case you're not cautious with this your endeavors to make and assemble compatibility will reverse discharge leaving your "subject" feeling that you're some way or another attempting to remove the mickey from them and you resembling an irritating dolt.

NLP has numerous utilizations in business and one of the key uses is to pick up impact over others.

How might you want to have the option to impart in a manner that empowered you to handily communicate as the need should arise to individuals at all various degrees of an association? How might you want to have the option to propel somebody to accomplish something just by your utilization of explicit language designs? How might you want to have the option to assist individuals with beating their issues so as to make them progressively proficient and profitable? How might you like to have the option to impact client decisions by speaking with them at an oblivious level so they simply get a positive sentiment about your item or support and acknowledge your proposals?

NLP can assist you in doing the entirety of this. Our NLP Practitioner arrangement of instructional classes is accessible as an e-Learning bundle or we can convey the preparation in-house to suit you.

How can it work? All things considered, NLP instructs you that we as a whole have certain inclinations by the way we think, how we speak to the world to ourselves. On the off chance that we can comprehend the manner in which that we figure, at that point, we can impact how we think.

For instance. We as a whole have a favored framework for deciphering what goes on in our lives into our contemplations. We either like to utilize our feeling of sight, sound, or contact. On the off chance that we have a favored feeling of sight, at that point we will interpret effectively what we experience into pictures in our mind. On the off chance that we have a favored feeling of touch, at that point we will handily make an interpretation of that into inner sentiments and so forth.

On the off chance that we have an inclination for contact, at that point we may make statements like "look you up some other time," "you can clutch that idea," "I get a nice sentiment when I think about that" all expressions that include a physical feeling of touch or feeling.

Along these line, on the off chance that we know this, at that point, we can tune in to what individuals state, and we can determine what their favored mechanism of correspondence is. We can increase the oblivious impact over them by utilizing their favored arrangement of correspondence back to them. Thus, we will utilize words and expressions that they use so as to do this. Clever eh?

Have you seen that individuals like individuals who resemble them? Do you and your companions have normal interests? This is the way it works.

Give this a shot when you are conversing with them again. Watch their shoulders go here and there as they breathe in and out, and duplicate them. Along these lines, when they breathe in, you breathe in, when they breathe out, you breathe out. Notice how it gives you an oblivious association with them. They won't recognize what you have done yet they will feel increasingly associated with them and they will like you all the more subliminally.

Chapter 15:   Emotions

You must be able to recognize how emotions sway other people, why we have them, and how to sway them if you want to be able to control people. This is for one key reason—emotions are motivating. They drive everything. Once you understand how people are feeling, you can begin to recognize how your own behaviors influence the feelings of others. Once you understand that, you can tweak your own behaviors intentionally in order to evoke the desired behavior from the other person. The more control you gain over another's emotions, the more control you have over their thoughts and behaviors. This is because thoughts, feelings, and behaviors work together in a constant, never-ending cycle. Your thoughts influence your feelings, and your feelings influence your behaviors, which in turn, continue the cycle.

What are Emotions?

Ultimately, emotions are somewhat simple to define in theory. Despite how vastly different they may be from each other; all emotions have some base similarities at their foundation. In particular, they have three key features that define what they are. They are natural, they are reflexive, and they are instinctive.

In being natural, they come on their own. They were created over millennia of evolution and development, forming in ways that would be conducive to the survival of life as life continued to grow more and more complex over time. The more complex and capable of thought life grew, the more emotional capacity was necessary to control them.

Emotions are reflexive, meaning they are reactions to the world around them. If left completely unprovoked with no real stimulus, emotional states do not change much. Things happen around you to sway you into feeling one way or the other. For example, getting hurt can cause negative feelings of sadness, anger, or fear. This is because all three of those emotions can aid in survival in that particular situation—sadness lends itself to getting the support of others. Anger lends itself to defending oneself, and fear lends itself to flee. When emotions are reflexive, they are meant to bolster one's chances at survival.

Lastly, emotions are instinctive. They happen automatically with very little thought involved. They do not require much conscious thought to arise, instead of happening on their own. This is largely believed to be due to the fact that humans have two different thought processes that operate largely independently from each other. Humans have the implicit or automatic thought process, which involves instinctive judgments and behaviors, such as emotions, and they have the explicit or controlled thought process that is responsible for rational thought, learning, and development. Emotions fall into the implicit, unconscious thought process—they occur on their own without feeling the constraints of rationality.

Of course, when they are not constrained by rationality, it is easy to understand how fickle they can be—emotions can largely be influenced by several different external factors. Anything from how the day went to what you ate could sway your emotions.

Why We Have Emotions

Despite how fickle and impractical emotions can be, they have important biological purposes. If they were not important, they would not have developed over the course of several thousands of years in a wide range of species. Many animals with higher brain development have the areas in the brain believed to be responsible for different emotions—it is not solely a human thing. With that in mind, the two biggest purposes for emotions are survival and communication with a crowd.

As briefly touched upon, emotions are reflexive. They are natural, instinctive responses to the world around you meant to boost your survival. This is because they are motivators. Emotions motivate you to perform certain actions and behaviors in hopes of firstly surviving and secondly passing on genes to the next generation. Because you will naturally and instinctively feel certain ways when exposed to certain situations, your own behaviors will be influenced. If something makes you scared, you are likely to approach it cautiously or avoid it altogether. This is because fear serves to put your body on high alert. If something makes you happy, you are likely going to continue to seek exposure to it because happiness is what is felt when needs are met, and means you are doing something right. Of course, this is not always necessarily an accurate way to go about life, but it is a good rule of thumb. Things that trigger happiness, such as love, affection, sex, good food, and rest are all generally good for survival.

Secondarily, emotions serve as a major component for effective communication. When you can communicate effectively, you are better able to survive. You will be able to clearly iterate whatever it is you need in that particular moment simply because emotions are all about your current unconscious thoughts, feelings, and needs revolving whatever is happening around you. Those feelings trigger specific reactions in the body, namely in body language, actions, and expressions, and those three things culminate into a way to nonverbally communicate your needs to those around you. Those who are closest to you are likely to then want to behave in ways that are beneficial to you, actively seeking to meet your needs to ensure you are cared for simply because they understand that you have needs as well. Further, when you can read the needs of others around you, you can also choose to regulate your own behavior. Think of anger, for example—it is largely an alarm emotion. You feel anger when you feel as though you are being wronged or your boundaries have been overstepped. When you feel angry, you will show the typical angry body language. When someone else sees that their own actions have made you angry, they then have the opportunity to tweak their

own behaviors to ensure they do not continue to make you feel wronged. Both of these facets of communication aid in the survival of the social species. Because humans naturally crave living in groups of people, surrounded by others, they need to have a good understanding of the thoughts and feelings of those around them in order to live in a happy, healthy manner without angering everyone.

What Emotions Say

We have dozens of emotions—joy may be different than exuberance, for example, and disappointed is different than agony. While they may fall under similar categories of emotions—such as joy and exuberance both falling under the umbrella category of happiness and agony and disappointment both falling, at least in part, under sadness—they are different. Rather than going through each emotion step-by-step to define it, we will look at broader categories. The seven emotions that will be presented here are believed to be the seven fundamental emotions, meaning that all emotions felt will fall under the category of one or several of the emotions listed here. Emotions exist on a spectrum, and they can be quite complex, particularly when you start feeling complicated, conflicting feelings, and for that reason, reducing the wide range of feelings down to the seven universal feelings that are known to occur in all cultures across the world, no matter how distanced or withdrawn the people may be. Each of these seven emotions evokes a specific facial expression in response that can be recognized across cultures. Even people that are born blind and never get to see expressions exhibit the expressions that go along with these seven emotions, making them believed to be universal.

Anger

Anger is felt like a response to something wronging the individual or overstepping a boundary. It is meant to evoke protection or defensive behavior and conveys a deep need for a boundary to be respected or some distance to be given.

Fear

Fear is felt during times of active threat. The individual believes that he or she is in danger, and the body responds to that by preparing to either fight or flee to survive. When seeing this emotion in others, it conveys a need for security and safety.

Contempt

Contempt is felt when an individual feels a deep hatred or disapproval for another person or thing. It is usually caused as a response to not believing in something someone is saying or lacking trust or respect for the other person. It conveys a need for trust.

Disgust

Disgust is usually felt when you are exposed to something that is toxic to your health. It is usually reserved for things that will make you ill if you consume it, but it can also be directed toward people as well if they have done something utterly against your moral code. It usually conveys that whatever is present is toxic and should be avoided at all costs.

Happiness

Happiness is the ultimate sign that you are doing everything right and should continue to do so. It means that the individual is satisfied during that moment and that all needs are met. It is pleasant and meant to encourage the individual to continue doing whatever evoked that happiness response in the first place.

Sadness

Sadness is felt in times of pain or loss. It triggers a withdrawal in which the individual feeling sadness attempts to escape from the cause of the pain or the loss and is a cue that major support is needed in order to heal.

Surprise

Surprise occurs when something startling or unexpected has occurred. It usually means that something that did not line up with prior belief sets has occurred and that it requires further attention in order to understand what has happened.

Chapter 16: Deception

How would you feel if you found out that someone who's been a good friend has been deceiving you all along? You would obviously feel betrayed, deceived, and foolish. In as much as we try to be very careful in life, the truth is that we will definitely come across people who will deceive us into believing a total falsehood or pretend to be someone who they are not.

Recently, in the United States, there was a viral news story of a man who pretended to be deaf and dumb for 65 years in order to avoid listening to his wife's drama. He successfully deceived her for 65 years until he was finally caught. This is exactly one thing every deceptive person needs to remember; the fact that you cannot deceive a person forever. Either the person you are deceiving finds out or the entire thing ends in shambles. Whichever way, the victim ends up not trusting the agent or anyone at all. The victim becomes insecure and begins to question every action of the agent.

Types of Deception

Lies: This is the most common type of deception usually exhibited by deceptive people. A lot of people find out that, they have been lied to by the people they hold in high esteem or by the people they actually love. This happens when someone decides to tell you something that is a total falsehood or fallacy. Information that is completely far from the truth is given to deceive other people for reasons best known to the agent. Sometimes, people who tell lies do not even have a genuine reason for doing so; it could be because the agent wishes to hide his past or wants to stop you from getting access to important information. Other times, people deceive other people by lying to them in order to make the subject respect them or think highly of them. The deceptive person is the only person who knows the reasons behind the lies he tells you.

Exaggerations: This is a type of deception which takes place when the agent adds to a story or tells a story in an exaggerated manner. This isn't always completely a lie; it is only a story that has been rephrased and re-ordered. It is the act of elevating the truth. For instance, when someone asks if you have ever been to Paris when you haven't and you reply "I have been there so many times." Many deceptive people use this method a lot and when confronted, they would confidently say that they didn't exactly deceive you or lie to you. However, it doesn't change the fact that a lie is a lie whether exaggerated or not.

Understatements: This is the act of downplaying the truth. An understatement isn't too far from the truth but it is a form of deception because it is not the "truth." Anything that isn't the truth is a "lie". This form of deception is something everyone has done at one point or the other. If you have ever told your parents you purchased an item at a price "below" the actual price, you have understated the truth. When you tell your friend you didn't invite them to your party because it was a "little get together" (when it was actually an elaborate party), you have downplayed the truth. Understatement doesn't actually qualify as a "lie" but since the motive behind the use of understatements often turns out to restrict the subject from being aware of some things, it automatically makes it a type of deception.

Concealment: This is the act of omitting some information, holding back, or refusing to disclose some of the truth. Often times, people who use this type of deception do so in order to leave out some details or omit certain details. These details may be really important. Sometimes, a person may decide to use this method because he doesn't want you to know certain things about him. The information he's trying to hide may reveal his identity or his flaws, so he decides to leave these details out in order to make you believe he's innocent.

Equivocation: This is the act of using ambiguous statements or confusing statements. This type of deception practically leaves the subject confused because the statement is unclear and indirect. It gives no direct meaning and may actually have more than one meaning.

Understanding the Motives of Deceptive People

In every human relationship, human beings deceive each other for reasons best known to them. Nevertheless, the three most popular motives used for deception are:

Partner focused motive: This motive of deception is one that isn't selfish at all. On the other hand, it is used when the agent seeks to protect the agent against certain things or people. What do we mean by this? Have you ever been in a situation where someone said something really bad about your loved one and you flared up so much but refused to tell your loved one anything? You choose not to tell, because you probably do not want them getting into a fight or feeling bad over what the other person said. This is exactly the idea of this motive. Although your partner may flare up if they found out, they would come to understand you did it in their best interest. Not every single motive of deception is actually bad, an example of one is this; the partner focused motive. The aim is meant for protecting the subject and it is often in the best interest of the subject. Sometimes, when the subject finds out, they might lose some trust in the agent, regardless of the good intentions behind the deception. They begin to wonder if the agent has other information they aren't disclosing as well. This is why deception isn't recommended at all; it has successfully ruined several relationships.

Self-focused motive: This motive of deception is a completely self-centered and conceited one, although the agent may try to justify his reasons in several ways. This is when the agent deceives the subject in a bid to protect himself or carry out his own selfish desires. When people chose to deceive other people for selfish reasons like "suiting their ego," pretending to be who they are not, and for the purpose of avoiding trouble. Sometimes, the agent deceives the subject in order to create an impression. These types of people do not care about the feelings of the subject and do not care about what happens, when the subject eventually discovers the truth. Often times, when the subject finds out the truth, they break down feeling emotionally betrayed and deceived. However, some deceptive people are very good at what they do and can easily defend themselves by either coming up with another lie or telling the subject what they want to hear. The agent is always well acquainted with his subject and is often aware of his subject's weaknesses. This allows him to bail his way out when caught or found out. Whichever way, the subject ends up finding it difficult to trust other people.

Relationship focused motive: In this case, the motive of the agent is to protect his relationship with the subject. This is when the agent conceals certain information from the subject in order to avoid destroying the relationship. Sometimes, a cheating partner may lie in a relationship because they do not want to risk their partner leaving them. They do not want their partner to find out because they are not ready to bear the consequences of their actions. Sometimes, the agent feels guilty but he would rather keep the information to himself because he knows it's not good for the relationship.

Chapter 17:   Manipulation

What is Manipulation?

The fundamental solicitation that is consistently introduced is what control is? At the present time will talk about control in the focal points of mental control, which is a social impact that attempts to change the practices or impression of others, or the subject, through cruel, beguiling, or insightful procedures. The controller is quitting any and all funny business to move their own one of sort inclinations, by and large to the disadvantage of another, so most by a wide margin of their frameworks would be viewed as misleading, naughty, harming, and exploitative. While social impact itself isn't continually negative, when an individual or get-together is being controlled, it has the authenticity of causing them to hurt.

Social impact, for example, by ethical of an authority attempting to convince their patients to begin getting sound affinities, is regularly seen to be something that is innocuous. This is considerable for any social impact that is fit for as to help those included to pick and isn't unduly coercive. Obviously, if someone is trying to get their own specific way and is using people without expecting to, the social impact can be hazardous and is all around looked plummeting on.

Mental or energized control is viewed as a sort of effect and motivation. There are different portions that can be joined into this sort of mind control, for example, tormenting and brainwashing. Generally, people will consider this to be coldblooded or puzzling in nature. The people who choose to use control will do in that limit so as to endeavor to control the direction of everybody around them. The controller will have some outrageous objective as a top need and will work through different abuse frameworks to constrain people around them into helping the controller locate a serviceable pace objective. Routinely fiery shakedown will be fused.

The people who practice control will use mind control, brainwashing, or annoying systems to get others to finish the undertakings for them. The subject of the controller most likely won't have any desire to play out the errand, yet feel that they have no other option because of the compulsion or other philosophy used. Most by a long shot who are manipulative don't have the most ideal minding and affectability towards others so they may not see an issue with their activities.

Different controllers need to locate a serviceable pace objective and are not worried over who has been vexed or harmed on the way. Essentially, manipulative people are a significant part of the time reluctant to get into a strong relationship since they are frightful others won't remember them. Someone who has a manipulative character will routinely have the failure to anticipate hazard for their own practices, issues, and life. Since they are not set up to anticipate the hazard for these issues, the controller will use the procedures of control to get someone else to acknowledge control over the obligation.

Controllers are a significant part of the time arranged to use relative frameworks that are found in different sorts of mind control so as to get the impact they need over others. One of the most usually used frameworks is known as excited coercion. This is the detect the controller will work to rouse compassion or fault in the subject they are controlling. These two estimations are picked since they are viewed as the two most grounded of every human inclination and are the well while in travel to spike others into the action that the controller needs. The controller will by then have the choice to abuse the subject, using the compassion or accuse that they have made to pressure others into arranging or helping them appear at their last objective.

Sometimes, the controller won't just have the choice to make these opinions, they will have the decision to rouse degrees of sympathy or accuse that are way out of degree for the situation that is going on. This proposes they can take a condition, for example, abandoning a party appear as though the subject is deserting an internment administration or something that is enormous.

A fiery investigation is only one of the methods that are used by controllers. One of the different methods that have been gainful for specific, controllers is to use a kind of misuse that is known as insane making. This strategy is usually pointed with the drive for making self-question in the subject being controlled; as regularly as possible this self-defenselessness will wind up being reliable to the point that a few subjects may start to have feelings that they are going crazy. Now and again, the controller will use sorts of isolated directing behavior to recognize insane making. They may in like way show backing or endorsing of the subject verbally, yet then offer non-verbal hints that show confining ramifications. The controller will routinely effectively try to undermine certain occasions or practices while displaying their help so anybody can hear for that equivalent lead. In the event that the controller is trapped in the appearing, they will use repudiation, sponsorship, defend, and cheating of incapacitated course of action so as to escape from the issue.

Possibly the best issue with mental controllers is that they are not continually arranged to perceive what others around them may need, and they will lose the capacity to address or much thinks about these issues. This doesn't exculpate the immediate that they are doing, yet regularly the essentials of others are not considered or are not a need to the controller so they can perform manipulative undertakings without feeling fault or disapproval. This can make it difficult to stop the direct and clarify in a commonplace manner why the controller must stop.

Besides, the controller may find that it is difficult for them to shape significant and dependable family relationships and associations because the people they are with will dependably feel externalized and will experience issues in confiding in the controller. The issue goes the two novel courses in the strategy of associations; the controller won't have the decision to see the necessities of the other individual while the other individual won't have the decision to shape the basic enthusiastic affiliations or trust with the controller.

Necessities to Successfully Manipulate

A profitable controller must have methods near to that will make them beneficial at using people to locate a decent pace last objective. While there are two or three speculations on what makes a practical controller, we will investigate the three necessities that have been set out by George K. Simon, an effective psychology producer. As demonstrated by Simon, the controller should:

1. Be arranged to cover their convincing practices and wants from the subject.

2. Be arranged to pick the vulnerabilities of their typical subject or on the other hand, abused people to comprehend which techniques will be the best in appearing at their destinations.

3. Have some degree of mercilessness rapidly accessible, so they won't have to manage any doubts that may arise because of hurting the subjects if it wraps up that way. This damage can be either physical or excited.

The fundamental that the controller needs to achieve all together to sufficiently control their subjects is to conceal their convincing practices and targets. If the controller evades telling everyone their game-plans or dependably acts intend to other people, nobody will remain adequately long to be controlled. Or on the other hand, maybe, the controller ought to have the option to cover their musings from others and act like everything is normal. Consistently, the people who are being controlled won't get it, at any rate for no situation. The controller will be sweet, act like their closest companion, and potentially help them with a trip with some issue or another. When the subject ponders the issue, the controller has enough information on them to oblige the subject into progressing forward.

Next, the controller should have the limit of comprehending what the vulnerabilities of their organized awful misfortune or abused people are. This can assist them with making sense of which methods should be used so as to appear at the general objective. A portion of the time the controller may have the decision to do this development through a touch of recognition while different occasions they are going to need to have a sort of relationship with the subject before thinking of the full arrangement.

The third need is that the controller should be barbarous. It won't turn out positively if the controller places in the aggregate of their work and, by then stresses how the subject is going to reasonable at last. If they considered the subject, it isn't likely that they would continue with this strategy in any capacity whatsoever. The controller won't consider the subject at all and doesn't generally mind if any damage, either physical or lively, happens to the subject as long as the general objective is met.

One clarification that controllers are so convincing is that the subject as often as conceivable doesn't grasp they are being controlled until some other time simultaneously. They may feel that everything is coming alright; maybe they envision that they have made another accomplice in the controller. When the subject remembers they are being used or never again ought to be a touch of the method, they are gotten. The controller will have the choice to use a wide extent of strategies, including vivacious shakedown, to get their direction at last.

Chapter 18: Strategies to Detect and Ward Off Manipulation

There are different strategies you can use to identify manipulative people. There are such people in your immediate environment, in your family, but also in your circle of friends and acquaintances and at work. The closest companion is the partner. If you have the feeling that influence is being exerted on you undercover from this environment, you can uncover and counteract manipulation with various defense mechanisms.

Pay Attention to Questionable Procurement of Information

When you are conducting conversations, pay close attention to how the conversation is presented. If it takes the form of an interview, so that the communication is very one-way, the person you are talking to wants to learn more about you and gather information. The information is then used to manipulate you and take you in the desired direction.

For this to succeed, the other person must gain knowledge of your strengths and weaknesses. A good manipulator is characterized by his supposed strengths. He knows very well how to hide his weaknesses. Your weaknesses are used by him to influence you, no matter whether this results in damage for you in the end. But there are good possibilities to fight against sounding out. If you feel that the communication is too one-sided, try to turn the tables and find out more about yours.

A successful interview is based on mutual exchange and does not become an interview. Only try to reveal things in the interview that the interviewer should know about and don't let him or her influence you to go deeper into your thinking and emotions to find out more. Steer the conversation in a different direction by asking many questions or countering with counter-questions. In the best case, you create the feeling in your conversation partner that he or she is not learning anything about you. This defuses the situation.

Truths with A False Bottom

People who want to manipulate their way of thinking do not take the truth so seriously.

Stories are told that never happen or are only half the truth. Often these people are so good at it that the information is not directly recognized as half-truth or lies. This is because manipulators do not have a guilty conscience when they build up a story that serves their purpose. But lies can be exposed quickly. Because the interlocutor needs an explanation if he or she asks targeted, apparently trivial questions. He or she answers excessively and tries to justify himself or herself effusively.

Especially situations that scratch the image of the liar and put him in the wrong light need a special presentation from his point of view. There are special situations where liars immediately attract attention. A good example of this is the accusation of not acting fairly but selfishly or criticism on the job.

If you feel that you are facing dubious truths, disarm that person with questions. If there are no answers at all or only evasive answers and nervousness sets in, you can assume that you have just caught a liar. Further, more specific questions will even make your retreat.

Take A Closer Look at The Exaggerated Charm

One of the greatest weapons of manipulators is excessive charm. Therefore, you should take a closer look at whether the charming appearance is in keeping with your temperament or is just an act to flatter you and learn more about you. You can recognize manipulators by the following indications:

- Before a request is made, you will receive compliments.

- Favors are only done in situations where there is an advantage for the person.

- Certain gestures are only used for personal benefit.

- Charm is only used when the situation promises advantages.

- These people are less charming in other, non-advantageous situations.

If these points are true, you are dealing with a person who is charming for selfish reasons. It is not an honest, sincere charm, but a superficial behavior that is only used for self-interest. Such people are dazzlers, and you should not be fooled by them.

Therefore, observe and question the motives for their charming behavior. Charming behavior should not be linked to conditions, just as a favor you do for someone should not be linked to conditions. Just say "no" once when a person with charm ensnares you and then wants something from you. Superficial charm quickly takes advantage of your good nature because the clear view is clouded.

Role Patterns Give A Very Deep Insight

Manipulators present themselves as martyrs and are seen as good-natured, helping, self-sacrificing people who do everything right. These apparent sacrifices made by the person evoke compassion and sympathy in others, which only serves to manipulate another person. People who want to manipulate quickly recognize the weaknesses of other people and use them to blackmail you emotionally. Because they know what causes you pain, with targeted criticism, they evoke a feeling of inferiority and scratch your self-confidence.

The result of this situation is a feeling of emotional obligation, so you push yourself into the role of having to prove something to yourself. An alleged basis of trust can also be an indication of a certain role pattern that ultimately amounts to manipulation. A good example is a secret that is entrusted to you, which is later linked to a certain favor. Here you can be sure that this person wants to manipulate you and use you for his benefit. Make sure that telling the secret is only to learn more about you. This information is guaranteed to be used against you later.

If you do not fulfill the intended role, you will be ignored or even punished with contempt and ignorance. If someone else wants to impose this role on you, where compassion is the main thing and favors are demanded of you, you should say "no". Favors are always for unselfish reasons. Manipulative people play with your emotions and try to elicit secrets from you by making you feel guilty. The best way to recognize role patterns is to observe, to express your opinion and not to trust hastily.

Check That Your Decisions Are Free from Manipulation

People who want to manipulate are characterized by the fact that they influence the opinions and decisions of others. To recognize manipulation, you have to take a closer look at and reflect on your freedom of decision. You can do this with the following questions:

- Has the decision been made without the intervention of others?

- Has external pressure been exerted during the decision-making process?

- Is your opinion strongly influenced by another person?

- Are there fears that someone may be disappointed by their decision?

- Are there consequences if your opinion should not be different?

If you answer "yes" to these questions, your freedom of choice is influenced by a manipulative person and no longer corresponds to your emotions and needs.

These are employed at the back and are not considered. For the manipulator, his well-being and goal are paramount. Everything else falls by the wayside.

Important: No one has the right to make decisions over your head. You should trust your judgment. If you consider a decision to be right and good, assert yourself without restrictions. Your common sense will guide you correctly. Just because someone insists on their right does not mean that your decision is wrong. Through reflection, you can see the basis on which your decision is based. If the arguments are convincing, you should not deviate from your opinion or decision and not allow yourself to be influenced.

Chapter 19: Identifying Lies

Fact is that only 54% of the lies can be spotted in an accurate manner. Research has also proved that extroverts tell more lies when compared to the introverts and not less than 82% of the lies usually go without being detected.

However, the good news is that people can also improve their abilities for lie detection, maximizing to close to 90% accuracy. The big question here is how to detect that someone is lying. One of the initial steps in this whole process is getting with how someone typically acts, especially when they are speaking.

Basically, this is the process of coming up with known as a baseline. A baseline is essentially how a person acts when they are under non-threatening and just normal conditions. According to the Science of People website, it is basically how a person appears when they are saying the truth. To make it clearer, it might be a bit difficult to tell when a person is not speaking the fact if you are not sure of how they usually act when saying the truth, which, to a wider extent, makes a lot of sense.

However, the techniques that are used to determine if someone is lying can be very confusing. As a matter of fact, these strategies can even be very conflicting. Due to that, it is important to think twice before making an accusation, ensure that you feel more than once about doing it unless it is important to go ahead and find out what happened.

Here are some of the telltale signs that someone is not telling the truth;

The Behavioral Delay or Pause

It begins when you ask someone a question, and you get no reply initially. The person then begins to respond after some delay. There is one big issue that ought to be asked here; to what extent the deferral should reach out before it gets important and before it tends to be viewed as a deceptive sign? It, however, depends on a few factors. You can try this particular exercise on a friend, and ask a question like this, "What were you doing on a day like this six years ago.

After asking that question, you will notice that the person will take an invariable pause before answering the question. This is because it is not a type of question that naturally evokes a fast and immediate answer. Even as the person takes time to think about the question, he might still not be able to give a meaningful response. The next question to ask would be this," Did you rob a cloth shop on this day six years ago?" if they make a pause before giving you the answer you need, then it would be very important to pick the kind of friends you have wisely.

In most cases, there will be no pause, and the person is likely to respond by just saying no and letting the story die.

This is a simple test that tends to drive home the point that the delays should usually be considered out of the church of God. in the context of whether; it is appropriate for the question at hand.

The Verbal or Non-Verbal Disconnect

The human brains have been wired in a manner that causes both the nonverbal and the verbal behaviors to match up in a natural manner. So, each time, there is a disconnect, it is usually regarded as a very important deceptive indicator. A very common verbal or nonverbal disconnect that you should look out for will occur when someone nods affirmatively while giving a "No" answer.

It might also occur when a person moves his head from one end to the other when giving a "Yes" answer.

If you were to carry out that mismatch, as an example, to offer a response to a question, then you will realize that you will have to force yourself through the motion that you have. But despite all that, someone who is deceptive will still do it without even giving it a second thought.

There are a number of caveats that have been connected to this type of indicator. First of all, this type of indicator is not applicable in a short phrase or one-word response. Instead, it is only suitable in a narrative response. For instance, consider that a human head might make a quick nodding motion when a person says "No." That is just a simple emphasis and not a disconnect. Second, it is also very important not to forget that a nodding motion does not necessarily mean "Yes' in certain cultures. In such cultures, a side-to-side head motion also does not imply that the person is saying "No."

Hiding the Eyes or The Mouth

Deceptive people will always hide their eyes or mouth when they are not saying the truth. There is a tendency to desire to cover over a given lie, so if the hand of a person moves in front of their mouth while they are making a response to a given question, which becomes significant.

In a similar instance, hiding the eyes can be an inclination to shield a person from the outlast of those they could be lying to. If an individual shield or covers their eyes when they are responding to a question, what they could also be showing, on the level of subconscious, is that they can't bear to see the reaction to the lie they are saying. In most cases, this kind of eye shielding could be done using the hand, or the person could as well decide to close the eyes. Blinking is not in the picture here, but when a person closes their eyes while making a response to a question that doesn't need reflection to answer, which can be considered as a way of hiding the eyes, hence becoming a possible deceptive indicator.

Swallowing or Throat Clearing

If a person loudly swallows saliva or clears the throat before answering a given question, then there is a problem somewhere. However, if any of these actions are performed after they have answered the question, then there is nothing to worry about. But when it happens before answering a question, then there are some things that should be analyzed.

The Hand-to-Face Actions

The other way of determining if someone is saying a lie is to check what they do with their faces or in the head region each time they are asked a question. Usually, this would take the form of licking or biting the lips or even pulling the ears or lips together. The main reason behind this reflects one of the simple science questions that are usually discussed in high school. When you have someone a question, and you notice that it creates a kind of spike in anxiety, what you should remember is that the right response will be damaging. In return, that will activate the autonomic nervous system to get to business and try to dissipate the anxiety, which might appear to drain a lot of blood from the surface of the extremities, ears, and the face. The effects of this could be a sensation of itchiness or cold. Without the person even realizing it, his hands will be drawn to the mentioned areas, and there could be rubbing or wringing of the hands. And just like that, you might have spotted a deceptive indicator.

The Nose Touch

Women usually carry out this special gesture with smaller strokes compared to those of men, as a way of avoiding smudging of their make-ups. One of the most important things to recall is that this kind of action should be read in context and clusters, as the person could have any hay of cold or fever.

According to a group of scientists at the Smell & Taste Treatment and Research Foundation that is based in Chicago, when someone lies, chemicals that are called catecholamine are released and make the tissue that is inside the nose to swell. The scientists applied a special imaging camera that reveals the blood flow in the body and show that deliberate lying can also lead to an increase in the blood pressure. This technology proves that the human nose tends to expand with blood when someone lies, and that is what is referred to as the Pinocchio Effect.

Maximized blood pressure will also inflate the nose and make the nervous nose tingle, leading to a kind of brisk rubbing with the hand to suppress the itching effect.

The swelling cannot be seen with the naked eyes, but it is usually what causes the nose touch gesture. The same phenomenon will also take place when a person is angry, anxious, and upset. American psychiatrist Charles Wolf and neurologist Alan Hirsch carried out a detailed analysis of the testimony of Bill Clinton to the Grand Jury on the affair he had with Monica Lewinsky. They realized that each time he was being honest, he rarely touched his nose. However, when he lied, he offered he appeared to be wearing a frown before he gave the answer and touched his nose once each 4 minutes for a mega total of 26 nose touches. The scientists also said the former US president didn't touch his nose at all when he offered the answers to the questions in a truthful manner.

A deliberate scratching or rubbing action, as opposed to a nose that could just be itching lightly, usually satisfies the itch of someone's nose. Usually, an itch is a repetitive and isolated signal and is out of context or incongruent with the general conversation of the person.

Eye Rub

When a child does not want to see something, the only thing they will do is to cover their eyes. They usually do this with both of their hands. On the other hand, when an adult does not want to see something distasteful to them, they are likely to rub their eyes. The eye is one of the attempts by the brain to block out a doubt, deceit, or any distasteful thing that it sees. It is also done to avoid looking at the face of the person who the lie is being said to. Usually, men would firmly rub their eyes, and they may look away if the myth is a real whopper.

Women are not so likely to use the eye rub gesture. Instead, they will use gentle and small touching emotions just beneath the eyes since they either want to avoid interfering with the makeups they are wearing, or they have been redesigned as girls to stay away from making several gestures. At times, they might also want to avoid the listener's gaze by trying to look away.

One of the commonly used phrases out there is lying through the teeth. It is used to refer to a cluster of gestures portraying fake smile and clenched teeth, accompanied by the famous eye rub. It is a common gesture that is used by movie actors to show some level of dishonesty and by other traditions such as English, who will prefer not to say what they are exactly thinking.

Chapter 20:   Different Types of Liars

In the same way, there are different reasons why people tell lies. There are different types of liars too. Some people might lie because it is the easiest thing to do, while others might be sick. The following are three of the common types of liars you might encounter as you go about your day:

- Pathological Liars

- Sociopaths Liars

- Compulsive Liars

Let's take an in-depth look at each of these types so that we understand what makes them tick and how to identify them.

Pathological Liars

The scientific term for pathological lying is myth mania. You might already deduce from this that these are people whose lives revolve around myths. This is a habitual behavior to the point where it becomes a habit.

While most people can tell a white lie from time to time to prevent someone from getting hurt, pathological liars, on the other hand, don't need a reason to lie. Even when they don't have a reason to lie, they still do. Interacting with such people can be very difficult and frustrating because you are never sure whether to trust them or not.

Pathological liars tell tales that make them appear to be the hero of the situation or stories that evoke sympathy. There might not be anything for them to gain in telling a lie, but the attention matters to them anyway. The following are some of the characteristics that can help you identify a pathological liar:

Pointless Lies

Many people tell lies to get out of an uncomfortable situation or to avert a crisis or whichever reason. A pathological liar, on the other hand, is comfortable lying even when there is no clear benefit to the lie. It is very frustrating interacting with such people because even after you learn about the truth, you cannot reconcile their lie and any achievable gains.

Complicated Lies

One of the defining characteristics of pathological liars is the lengths they go to sell a lie. They create stories that are too complicated, dramatic, and have a lot of detail. This is possible because they are also very good at telling stories. Their tales might be compelling because of how good they can spin stories in an instant.

Victim or Hero Stories

Another thing that defines a pathological liar is their desire for attention. They must be at the center of the story. In this case, they will either be the victim in the story or the hero, but never the villain. People should either applaud them or sympathize with them, hence their tales. They also tell these stories to gain approval and validation from their audience.

Strong Belief in Their Tales

The problem with pathological liars is that as the lie grows, so does the liar's belief in it. Pathological liars are known to be deluded with their version of the truth. It gets to a point where they strongly believe their lives are the truth.

Different Versions of One Tale

A pathological liar is so creative that they need to make everyone believe in their stories by any means possible. As a result, they tap into their creativity to keep the audience entertained whenever they can. The problem with this is that they easily forget the previous details and, as a result, end up telling one story in different versions.

Quick Responses

We all love someone who can address our concerns as fast as possible. This is one of the traits of pathological liars. They will respond to any issues raised very fast. However, you might realize that their answers are vague, and instead of answering the question, they try to throw you off your line of thought.

Sociopathic Liars

The term sociopath sends chills down your spine. You might feel unsettled and afraid. There are very many descriptions that have been put forward for sociopaths, but they all agree on a few things; sociopaths lack moral capacity or standards, and they don't have a conscience, or if they do, it only exists to serve their needs.

To understand how sociopathic liars, operate, it is important that we take a deep look at the definition of sociopaths. Sociopaths can be identified in four groups:

Affective. Sociopaths can't empathize. They don't feel or show emotions at all. It is pointless expecting a sociopath to see things from your perspective or to care about what you feel concerning their actions.

Interpersonal. They cannot form deep connections with people when it comes to social interactions. Most of their interactions are superficial. It is very easy for a sociopath to put on a show to impress someone, but it is no more than a smokescreen. They are the embodiment of antisocial beings.

Antisocial. The basic construct of a sociopath is that they are immune to normal social tendencies. They believe they are all alone in the world.

Behavioral. The behavior of a sociopath is unpredictable. They are unreliable, cannot be trusted to set goals, or take responsibility for their actions. They can't even understand the responsibility for their actions, let alone owning up to them. They are also very impulsive.

Sociopathic liars are extreme in everything they do. This is one of the main reasons why you should be wary of them. They feel no pain or remorse. If they are out to hurt you, they will keep at it until they think they have gained as much pleasure from your pain as possible.

Other than the fact that they cannot feel emotions, they also have no desire to understand what their actions do to others. They are manipulative people and will never reveal emotions unless they do to trick you. There is always an explanation for that ill deed they subjected you to.

Their explanations are in such a way that you might even feel guilty and remorseful, yet you are the victim in the situation. The following are some of the characteristics of sociopathic liars:

Strained and Difficult Relationships. Sociopathic liars struggle to establish healthy bonds with people in their lives. Because of this, most of the relationships they are in are full of chaos and are always unstable.

No Empathy. Are you hoping for empathy from a sociopathic liar? You are looking in the wrong place. Lack of empathy is one of the defining traits that identify people with antisocial personality disorder. Because they cannot empathize, sociopathic liars are a very dangerous lot.

Dishonesty. Deceit and dishonesty come so easily to a sociopathic liar. If they are in trouble, it is easier to tell a lie than to admit the truth. They will also lie for any reason, as long as they can get what they want.

Gross Irresponsibility. Sociopathic liars tend to be highly irresponsible. From social obligations to financial prudence, they don't care about anything. They don't believe in recourse for their actions, and this is why most of them end up on the wrong side of the law.

Aggression. When interacting with a sociopathic liar, you should watch out for aggressive outbursts. This is someone who might not care what you feel, but they know what they want. If they can be aggressive and threaten you into submission, they will do it.

Manipulation. Sociopathic liars are master manipulators. Everything they do is about them. They can charm and seduce their way into your life, but all this is aimed at a personal gain or for their pleasure.

Hostility. Hostility is an interesting principle when discussing sociopathic liars. While they might not necessarily be hostile by nature, it is easy for them to create a hostile environment and have you as an active participant without your knowledge.

Affinity for Risky Behavior. Sociopathic liars are very dangerous, given their desire for risky behavior. They don't care about theirs or anyone else's comfort or safety.

Compulsive Liars

There is too much exaggeration in the world today. Social media has made it very easy for people to live fake lives. They try to portray themselves as something else, often opposite of who they truly are. Outright lies, distorted information, convenient truths, and half-truths—all these are common experiences you will come across today.

There is not much difference between compulsive liars and pathological liars. They both lie on impulse and will try to be as persuasive as possible. You might come across some literature that uses both terms interchangeably.

Compulsive lying is a situation where someone is used to lying that it becomes a habit. Even when they have no reason to lie, they still do. Compared to pathological liars, it is very easy to spot a compulsive liar. While pathological liars are creative and charming, compulsive liars try to get by. They spring a lie and hope it works. When they are lying, they will exhibit most of the common signs that someone is dishonest, like avoiding eye contact, breaking a sweat, or rambling over their words. They get anxious, especially at the slightest hint that you have them figured out.

Experts believe that compulsive lying is not necessarily a sign of psychosis. This is because most of the time, these individuals are not withdrawn from reality. Most of them can tell apart their lies from the truth. Many compulsive liars become what they are as a result of their immediate environment.

It is also possible that compulsive liars might spin tales to help them cope with previous trauma in their lives or lack of confidence and low esteem. Many of these are short-term approaches, which do not pan out well in the long-run. Keeping track of all the lies becomes a problem and stressful. There is also the risk of strained relationships if their lies unfold, and in some cases, they might have their day in court.

To be safe, you have to learn to treat liars with caution. While most of the things they say might be lies, they might also tell the truth from time to time. The challenge lies in distinguishing the difference between their lies and truths. This is where your ability to read people comes in handy.

Study their body language carefully over time, and you will learn to know the signs of trouble. You can also learn some of the subjects that they love to lie about and dig deeper to understand why, especially if these are people who are so close and dear to you. Understanding the context is important in helping you understand them and protect you from the impending risks. When dealing with liars, you must also try not to withdraw from reality. Irrespective of your affection toward them, you have to respect the fact that the lies will happen again. This is who they are, so try not to take things too personally. You can also recommend treatment for them, especially for liars whose plight is already diagnosed.

Conclusion

One major reason why people are interested in learning how to read body language and analyze people is to learn how to detect when someone is lying or manipulating them. This is a very understandable motivation for learning about this subject. However, it isn't as simple as being able to look at a tiny expression on someone's face or the way they move their hands and know immediately that they are lying about something. It's a bit more complicated than that, but definitely worth thinking about!

The best way to gauge a person's emotions or thoughts in the most accurate way possible is to look at how comfortable or uncomfortable they are in the moment. This spectrum of comfort and discomfort is much more reliable and important than just trying to read one expression and assume that it means something specific for every person you come across. Experts claim that people who lie (and therefore, likely feel guilty) have to walk around knowing that they are not being honest, and that this can make it hard to feel comfortable. In fact, oftentimes they are walking around with distress and tension that is visible to those who know how to spot it.

Trying to hide the fact that you're being deceptive puts a lot of stress on the brain as you struggle to come up with answers for questions that would have been easy to answer truthfully. When people are really comfortable talking to us, it's easy to tell when they are displaying signs of discomfort, which can indicate that they are not being truthful.

This means that your goal should be to get the person as comfortable as you can through building a rapport. Then you will be able to figure out how that person normally acts, or what their "baseline" of behavior and mood is. When you can familiarize yourself with the way a person appears and behaves when they aren't threatened or nervous, you can more accurately recognize when they are.

Although looking at things such as context and the situation is helpful and relevant in detecting lies, it can be used to approach every aspect of reading body language. For example, if you visit a social gathering and everyone there is chatting and having a great time, but there is one person in the corner with their head down, that person is going to stand out to you. They will probably come across as uncomfortable which will lead you to think that there is something going on with them. You may ask that person if there is something wrong with them. However, observing this exact same demeanor in a person at a hospital, for example, wouldn't raise any flags because people are often uncomfortable at hospitals.

Paying attention to someone's comfort level in a specific context offers you clues for the way they are feeling at that moment. When you're on a date with someone new and the person appears to be comfortable, you can probably assume that they like to be with you. If you are giving someone an interview for a job and the applicant looks confident and comfortable until you ask a question about their history with stealing, this is something to take note of. Although body language isn't a concrete or precise science, using some acquired knowledge in combination with your own common sense and observations about context and environment, can lead you to be pretty good at it. Then you can accurately assess what the people with you are thinking.

Most parts of our body are sending signals about what we desire or the way we feel, on a subconscious level that we often are not aware of. There are specific cues that can signal certain thoughts or ideas, but you must also keep in mind the spectrum of comfort or discomfort and remember that an isolated signal you pick up is far from the entire picture. Now let's look into some specific body parts and what signals they may be sending.

A lot of people assume that facial expressions are the most reliable or obvious indication of someone's thoughts or moods. But you should first realize, when thinking about reading someone's face, is that their facial expressions are not the most reliable gauge of their thoughts or feelings. There are a few body parts that are more honest than this, which you'll find out about soon, but let's focus on this one first. Most of us are taught starting at childhood that certain actions and facial expressions are meant for specific events or occasions, even if they are not genuine or what we really feel. This means that people give fake expressions all the time. But there are a few cues that you can still read from the face or head.

One simple body language cue to teach yourself about which isn't always easy to recognize, is a person's fake smile. A fake smile, such as one we give in social events because we "want" to be polite or because we "have" to be polite, is only visible on the mouth. Everyone knows how to do a fake smile, but not many of us realize that fake smiles do not reach our eyes. When we smile for real, our eyelids, eyebrows, and sometimes even the entire head is involved and moves upward.

Another method for recognizing when someone is growing uncomfortable is looking for pursed or tight lips on them. This can be seen in old videos of politicians admitting to something shameful, where their lips almost disappear as they give their confessions. This shows that they don't like to be saying what they are saying, and oftentimes, pursed lips show that someone is telling you only part of the truth.

These are only two simple techniques for recognizing what some facial expressions may mean, and they can reveal quite a bit about someone's true or false feelings. However, so many different variations exist that it can be more complicated than this, and as already mentioned, faces are not always reliable when it comes to body language. That's why you must pay just as much attention to the whole body, if not even more. What other body parts can you look at to tell how someone is thinking or feeling?

Although this isn't a body part that people often think about when it comes to reading people and analyzing body language, our arms are a huge part of expressing feelings and thoughts. A lot of gestures and expressions are trained or taught to us throughout life, like the fact that it's rude to point. Apart from these obvious social norms, there are some other considerations to make about arms when trying to read someone's moods. Look at how much room or space they are taking up with their arms, and also how high their arms are reaching.

Gestures that seem to defy gravity, no matter what body part it happens in, are typically positive. As soon as someone becomes interested, excited, or happy, their arms rise, their chins and heads go up, and even their feet or legs might start to bounce or point upward. A person's arms are especially versatile when it comes to reading this behavior. When we're happy or excited that our arm movements are unrestricted and we may raise them over our heads. A happy and energized person makes motions that go against gravity with their arms. This is easy to remember since someone feeling "up" means they are happy, while the opposite means that they feel the opposite. When someone is in a confident mood, they affirmatively swing their arms as they walk, while an insecure person will keep their arms restrained as if gravity is pulling them downward.

Gesturing is linked with speaking, and using more gestures as we talk can add fuel to our thinking and articulation. Try this out and you will notice that when you use your hands as you talk, you have a clearer mind and can find the words you're searching for more easily. Many people do this without even being aware of it, but consciously using it to your advantage will get you far.

If you hope to come across as authoritative or respectable to those you speak with, you should be conscious of the pitch of your voice. When we're nervous, we might talk too loudly, too quietly, too high or too low. This is a habit you should work on for maximizing good impressions. Before you are making a phone call or going into an interview, practice keeping your voice at an even pitch. Don't talk too loudly, too fast, or too unevenly, and you will send the message that you are confident and capable of whatever you're about to do.

If you are hoping to be more effective at storing important memories, try uncrossing your legs and arms as you listen. This can also be used to help people interact more in a meeting or conference. If you notice a lot of people are sitting with crossed legs or arms, encourage them to stand up, move around, and interact with the environment. This will automatically cause them to feel more engaged and involved, and all around more positive about the experience.

Now that you have a better understanding of body language and how it affects communication, as well as its ability to change your frame of mind, you'll need to use it in practice yourself and try to identify it in others as they interact. While there are many different facets involved with body language and interpreting its meaning it is a knowledge base that can be easy to learn if you continue to practice.

Don't get so caught up in the terminology that you forget how much of this is already planted in your subconscious. Many of us have this so ingrained that we take it for granted and forget that it is actually imbedded in our minds. We commonly watch people interact during most phases of our day, and if you think about it you are usually assessing or analyzing these people without even thinking about it. It's usually when force the issue that we over complicate the ability to do this naturally.